facttest dies pluu... te

bene coplacuit mihi

Ipse ihs erat incipiens quasi an

norum triginta ut putabatur filius

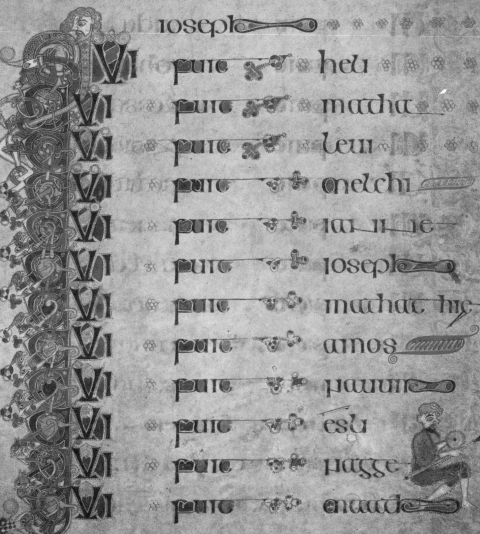

ioseph

VI fuit heli

VI fuit matthat

VI fuit leui

VI fuit melchi

VI fuit iannae

VI fuit ioseph

VI fuit mathat hie

VI fuit amos

VI fuit nauum

VI fuit eslu

VI fuit nagge

VI fuit enaud

For Mary Ellen
from James O'Doyle

How the
Irish Saved
Civilization

Big City Stories by Modern
American Writers (with Susan Cahill)

A Literary Guide to Ireland
(with Susan Cahill)

Jesus' Little Instruction Book

Looking for Books:
How to Find Hard to Find Books

how the Irish Saved Civilization

The Untold Story of Ireland's

Heroic Role from the Fall of Rome to the Rise of

Medieval Europe 🍂 Thomas Cahill

 Nan A. Talese DOUBLEDAY *New York London Toronto Sydney Auckland*

PUBLISHED BY NAN A. TALESE
an imprint of Doubleday, a division of
Bantam Doubleday Dell Publishing Group, Inc.
1540 Broadway, New York, New York 10036

DOUBLEDAY is a trademark of Doubleday, a division
of Bantam Doubleday Dell Publishing Group, Inc.

Page 237 constitutes an extension of this copyright page.

Book design by Marysarah Quinn

Maps and Illustrations by Martie Holmer

ENDPAPER

LEFT: LINDISFARNE GOSPELS

The beginning of the Christmas story in Matthew's Gospel, as contained in the Lindisfarne Gospels, completed in 698. Note the two languages: in red letters at the top of the page, we read the Latin, "Incipit evangelium secundum Mattheum" ("Here begins the Gospel according to Matthew"); above the Latin, in small, dark brown letters, a scribe has added a translation in early English, "Onginneth Godspell . . ." The rigidity of the subsequent letters derives from the example of Ogham, a primitive Irish form of the Latin alphabet, but the riot of stylized animals and other interlocking forms has its origins in prehistoric Irish art forms.

RIGHT: BOOK OF KELLS

This decorative page lists the genealogy of Jesus as found in Luke's Gospel. The scribe has left us a jaunty picture of himself—with palette and brush (and, for some reason, exposed private parts)—in the bottom right corner.

Library of Congress Cataloging-in-Publication Data
Cahill, Thomas.
    How the Irish saved civilization : the untold story of Ireland's heroic role from the fall of
    Rome to the rise of medieval Europe / Thomas Cahill. — 1st ed.
        p.   cm.
    Includes bibliographical references and index.
    1. Ireland—Civilization—To 1172.   2. Learning and scholarship—History—Medieval,
    500–1500.   3. Civilization, Classical—Study and teaching—Ireland.   4. Europe—
    Civilization—Irish influences.   5. Books—Ireland—History—400–1400.   6. Manuscripts
    —Ireland—History.   7. Monastic libraries—Ireland.   8. Transmission of texts.
    9. Scriptoria—Ireland.   I. Title.
    DA930.5.C34   1995
    941.501—dc20   94-28130
                                                                                CIP

ISBN 0-385-41848-5
Copyright © 1995 by Thomas Cahill

20 19 18 17

Nothing that is worth doing can be achieved in our lifetime; therefore we must be saved by hope. Nothing which is true or beautiful or good makes complete sense in any immediate context of history; therefore we must be saved by faith. Nothing we do, however virtuous, can be accomplished alone; therefore we must be saved by love.

—REINHOLD NIEBUHR

Table of Contents

Contents

Introduction

How Real Is History?

The word *Irish* is seldom coupled with the word *civilization*. When we think of peoples as civilized or civilizing, the Egyptians and the Greeks, the Italians and the French, the Chinese and the Jews may all come to mind. The Irish are wild, feckless, and charming, or morose, repressed, and corrupt, but not especially civilized. If we strain to think of "Irish civilization," no image appears, no Fertile Crescent or Indus Valley, no brooding bust of Beethoven. The simplest Greek auto mechanic will name his establishment "Parthenon," thus linking himself to an imagined ancestral culture. A semiliterate restaurateur of Sicilian origin will give pride of place to his plaster copy of Michelangelo's *David,* and so assert his presumed Renaissance ties. But an Irish businessman is far more likely to name his concern "The Breffni Bar" or "Kelly's Movers," announcing a merely local or personal connection, unburdened by the resonances of history or civilization.

And yet . . . Ireland, a little island at the edge of Europe that has known neither Renaissance nor Enlightenment—in some ways, a Third World country with, as John Betjeman claimed, a Stone Age culture—had one moment of unblemished glory. For, as the Roman Empire fell, as all through Europe matted, unwashed barbarians descended on the Roman cities, looting artifacts and burning books, the Irish, who were just learning to read and write, took up the great labor of copying all of Western literature—everything they could lay their hands on. These scribes then served as conduits through which the Greco-Roman and Judeo-Christian cultures were transmitted to the tribes of Europe, newly settled amid the rubble and ruined vineyards of the civilization they had over-whelmed. Without this Service of the Scribes, everything that happened subsequently would have been unthinkable. Without the Mission of the Irish Monks, who single-handedly re-founded European civilization throughout the continent in the bays and valleys of their exile, the world that came after them would have been an entirely different one—a world without books. And our own world would never have come to be.

Not for a thousand years—not since the Spartan Legion had perished at the Hot Gates of Thermopylae—had western civilization been put to such a test or faced such odds, nor would it again face extinction till in this century it devised the means of extinguishing all life. As our story opens at the beginning of the fifth century, no one could foresee the coming collapse. But to reasonable men in the second half of the century, surveying the situation of their time, the end was no longer in doubt: their world was finished. One could do nothing but, like Ausonius, retire to one's villa, write poetry, and await the inevitable. It never occurred to them that the building blocks of their world would be saved by outlandish oddities from a land so marginal that the Romans had not bothered to conquer it, by men so strange they lived in little huts on rocky outcrops and shaved half their heads and tortured themselves with fasts and chills and nettle baths. As Kenneth Clark said, "Looking back from the great civilizations of twelfth-century France or seventeenth-century Rome, it is hard to believe that for quite a long time—almost a hundred years—western Christianity survived by clinging to places like Skellig Michael, a pinnacle of rock eighteen miles from the Irish coast, rising seven hundred feet out of the sea."

Clark, who began his *Civilisation* with a chapter (called

"The Skin of Our Teeth") on the precarious transition from classical to medieval, is an exception in that he gives full weight to the Irish contribution. Many historians fail to mention it entirely, and few advert to the breathtaking drama of this cultural cliffhanger. This is probably because it is easier to describe stasis (classical, *then* medieval) than movement (classical *to* medieval). It is also true that historians are generally expert in one period or the other, so that analysis of the transition falls outside their—and everyone's?—competence. At all events, I know of no single book now in print that is devoted to the subject of the transition, nor even one in which this subject plays a substantial part.

In looking to remedy this omission, we may as well ask ourselves the big question: How real is history? Is it just an enormous soup, so full of disparate ingredients that it is uncharacterizable? Is it true, as Emil Cioran has remarked, that history proves nothing because it contains everything? Is not the reverse side of this that history can be made to say whatever we wish it to?

I think, rather, that every age writes history anew, reviewing deeds and texts of other ages from its own vantage point. Our history, the history we read in school and refer to in later life, was largely written by Protestant Englishmen and Anglo-Saxon Protestant Americans. Just as certain contemporary historians have been discovering that such redactors are not always reliable when it comes to the contributions of, say, women or African Americans, we should not be surprised to find that such storytellers have overlooked a tremendous contribution in the distant past that was both Celtic and Catholic, a contribution without which European civilization would have been impossible.

To an educated Englishman of the last century, for instance, the Irish were by their very nature incapable of civilization. "The Irish," proclaimed Benjamin Disraeli, Queen Victoria's beloved prime minister, "hate our order, our civilization, our enterprising industry, our pure religion [Disraeli's father had abandoned Judaism for the Church of England]. This wild, reckless, indolent, uncertain and superstitious race have no sympathy with the English character. Their ideal of human felicity is an alternation of clannish broils and coarse idolatry [i.e., Catholicism]. Their history describes an unbroken circle of bigotry [!] and blood." The venomous racism and knuckle-headed prejudice of this characterization may be evident to us, but in the days of "dear old Dizzy," as the queen called the man who had presented her with India, it simply passed for indisputable truth.

Occasionally, of course, even the smug colonists of the little queen's empire would experience a momentary qualm: Could the conquerors possibly be responsible for the state of the colonized? But they quickly suppressed any doubt and wrapped themselves in their impervious superiority, as in this response by the historian Charles Kingsley to the famine-induced destitution he witnessed in Victorian Ireland: "I am daunted by the human chimpanzees I saw along that hundred miles of horrible country. *I don't believe they are our fault* [emphasis mine]. I believe that there are not only many more of them than of old, but that they are happier, better and more comfortably fed and lodged under our rule than they ever were. But to see white chimpanzees is dreadful; if they were black, one would not feel it so much, but their skins, except where tanned by exposure, are as white as ours."

Nor can we comfort ourselves that such thinking passed

long ago from the scene. As the distinguished Princeton historian Anthony Grafton wrote recently in *The New York Review of Books* of history departments at the better American universities: "Catholic culture—like most Catholics—was usually disdained, as the province of lesser breeds fit only for the legendary parochial schools where nuns told their charges never to order ravioli on a date, lest their boy friends be reminded of pillows. Stereotypes and prejudices of this kind, as nasty as anything fastened upon Jews, persisted in American universities until an uncomfortably recent date."

That date may be only the day before yesterday. Yet this is not to accuse any historian of deliberate falsification. No, the problem is more subtle than deception—and artfully described by John Henry Newman in his fable of the Man and the Lion:

> The Man once invited the Lion to be his guest, and received him with princely hospitality. The Lion had the run of a magnificent palace, in which there were a vast many things to admire. There were large saloons and long corridors, richly furnished and decorated, and filled with a profusion of fine specimens of sculpture and painting, the works of the first masters in either art. The subjects represented were various; but the most prominent of them had an especial interest for the noble animal who stalked by them. It was that of the Lion himself; and as the owner of the mansion led him from one apartment into another, he did not fail to direct his attention to the indirect homage which these various groups and tableaux paid to the importance of the lion tribe.
>
> There was, however, one remarkable feature in all of them, to which the host, silent as he was from politeness,

seemed not at all insensible; that diverse as were these representations, in one point they all agreed, that the man was always victorious, and the lion was always overcome.

It is not that the Lion has been excluded from the history of art, but rather that he has been presented badly—and he never wins. When the Lion had finished his tour of the mansion, continues Newman, "his entertainer asked him what he thought of the splendours it contained; and he in reply did full justice to the riches of its owner and the skill of its decorators, but he added, 'Lions would have fared better, had lions been the artists.' "

In the course of this history, we shall meet many entertainers, persons of substance who have their story to tell, some of whom may believe that their story is all there is to tell. We shall be gracious and give them a hearing without disparagement. We shall even attempt to see things from their point of view. But every once in a while we shall find ourselves entertaining lions. At which moments, it will be every reader for himself.

We begin, however, not in the land of lions, but in the orderly, predictable world of Rome. For in order to appreciate the significance of the Irish contribution, we need first to take an inventory of the civilized empire of late antiquity.

I

The End of
the World

How Rome Fell
—and Why

On the last, cold day of December in the dying year we count as 406, the river Rhine froze solid, providing the natural bridge that hundreds of thousands of hungry men, women, and children had been waiting for. They were the *barbari*—to the Romans an undistinguished, matted mass of Others, not terrifying, just troublemakers, annoyances, things one would rather not have to deal with—non-Romans. To themselves they were, presumably, something more, but as the illiterate leave few records, we can only surmise their opinion of themselves.

Neither the weary, disciplined Roman soldiers, ranked along the west bank, nor the anxious, helter-skelter tribes amassing on the east bank could have been giving much thought to their place in history. But this moment of slack, this relative calm before the pandemonium to follow, gives us the chance to study the actors on both sides of this river and to look backward on what has been and forward to what will be.

Ascending heavenward like the Roman eagle, we can view the Rhine, widest river in Europe, rising out of Lake Constance in the northern Alps, bending and bowing north, then northwest, till after 820 miles of travel it reaches the coast of continental Europe and empties into the North Sea just opposite the Thames estuary. Returning to our Alpine heights, we can spot another river, rising from a smaller lake just north of Constance and coursing east for more than twice the length of the Rhine till it spends itself in the Black Sea. This is the Danube, Europe's longest river (after the Volga). To the north and east of these two Alpine rivers live the barbarians. To the south and west lies Romania, in its time the vastest and most powerful empire in human history.

The omnipotence and immensity of this empire—embracing, as it did, "the whole of the civilized world"—are not the qualities that would strike us were we to soar above the Mediterranean on that fateful day. What we would discern is the very opposite of power—fragility, specifically geographic fragility. "We live around a sea," the perspicacious Socrates had reminded his listeners, "like frogs around a pond." For all the splendor of Roman standard, the power of Roman boot, and the extent of Roman road, the entire empire hugs the Mediterranean like a child's village of sand, waiting to be swept into the sea. From fruitful Gaul and Britain in the north to the fertile Nile Valley in the south, from the rocky Iberian shore in the west to the parched coasts of Asia Minor, all provinces of the empire turn toward the great sea, toward Medi-Terra-nea— the Sea of Middle Earth. And as they turn to the center of their world, they turn their back on all that lies behind them, beyond the Roman wall. They turn their back on the barbarians.

That Rome should ever fall was unthinkable to Romans: its foundations were unassailable, sturdily sunk in a storied past and steadily built on for eleven centuries and more. There was, of course, the prophecy. Someone, usually someone in his cups, could always be counted on to bring up that old saw: the Prophecy of the Twelve Eagles, each eagle representing a century, leaving us with—stubby fingers counting out the decades in a puddle of wine—only seventy years remaining! Give or take a decade! Predictable laughter at the silliness of the whole idea. But in seventy years exactly, the empire would be gone.

Eternal Rome, eleven centuries old, hardly foresaw its doom. But theories about its fall are very old indeed. Two dozen years after this Roman-barbarian encounter along the Rhine, Augustine of Hippo, second city of Roman Africa, will be lying on his deathbed, listening to the clamor of another wave of barbarians as they attack the walls of his city. He has barely finished the final pages of his great defense of Christianity—*The City of God*—written to contradict the Roman pagans who discerned behind the barbarian assaults the old gods of Rome, angry at being forsaken by Christian converts. (No, insists Augustine eloquently, it is not Christianity but vice-encumbered paganism that is bringing the empire down.) Nine centuries later, as impressive feats of Roman engineering and sculpture are being dug up all over Italy at the dawn of the Renaissance, the question of what became of the cultural giants who built these things will be on everyone's lips. Petrarch, the Tuscan poet and scholar who is rightly remembered as the father of Renaissance humanism, rediscovers the concept of a "fall," which, following Augustine's lead, he blames on the empire's internal faults. Machiavelli, writing a century and a half later in a less spiritual, more cynical time, will blame the barbarians.

When the first volume of Edward Gibbon's *The History of the Decline and Fall of the Roman Empire* appeared in 1776, it raised far more lively interest in London than the news from the troublesome colonies in North America. "The decline of Rome," wrote Gibbon, "was the natural and inevitable effect of immoderate greatness." Such a perception fit well with the cool and rational temper of the time. But as the more conventional English gentlemen of the late eighteenth century continued to turn the pages of Mr. Gibbon's discourse, their blood began to boil. "As the happiness of a *future* life is the great object of religion," he continued, "we may hear, without surprise or scandal, that the introduction, or at least the abuse, of Christianity had some influence on the decline and fall of the Roman empire. The clergy successfully preached the doctrines of patience and pusillanimity; the active virtues of society were discouraged; and the last remains of the military spirit were buried in the cloister; a large portion of public and private wealth was consecrated to the specious demands of charity and devotion; and the soldiers' pay was lavished on the useless multitudes of both sexes, who could only plead the merits of abstinence and chastity."

Shock was registered and rebuttals issued, and Mr. Gibbon hastened to defend himself in his *Vindication*. But, in truth, his theory was no novelty, being scarcely distinguishable from the pagan theory Augustine had taken up the cudgels against more than thirteen centuries earlier. Nor was it devoid of merit. Still, it is helpful to know a little of Gibbon's own history: at sixteen, an intense convert to Catholicism, packed off to Switzerland by his outraged father, where he was reconverted to Protestantism (this time, of the Calvinist variety) and, almost simultaneously, to the uncompromising skepticism of Voltaire, whom he met. The permanent effect on the mature man of so many—and contradictory—youthful passions may easily be guessed.

These earlier interpreters—first the pagan critics of Christianity, then Augustine, Petrarch, Machiavelli, and Gibbon— have defined the limits of all later interpretation: Rome fell because of inner weakness, either social or spiritual; or Rome fell because of outer pressure—the barbarian hordes. What we can say with confidence is that Rome fell gradually and that Romans for many decades scarcely noticed what was happening.

Clues to the character of the Roman blindness are present

in the scene along the frozen Rhine. The legionnaires on the Roman bank know that they have the upper hand, and that they always will have. Even though some are only half-civilized recruits recently settled on this side of the river, they are now Romans, inheritors of nearly twelve centuries of civilization, husbandry, agriculture, viniculture, horticulture, cuisine, arts, literature, philosophy, law, politics, martial prowess—and all the "gear and tackle and trim" that goes with these pursuits. The world has never known anything as deep, as lasting, or as extensive as Pax Romana, the peace and predictability of Roman civilization. Inspecting the Roman soldiers now, we note the quiet authority of their presence, the polish of their person, the appropriateness of their stance—they are spiffy. More than this, there is an esthetic to each gesture and accoutrement. All details have been considered—*ad unguem,* as they would say, to the fingertip, as a sculptor tests the smoothness and perfection of his finished marble. Their hair is cut with a thought to the shape of the head, they are clean-shaven to show off the resoluteness of the jawline, their dress—from their impregnable but shapely breastplates to their easy-movement skirts—is designed with the form and movement of the body in mind, and their hard physiques recall the proportions of Greek statuary. Even the food in the mess is prepared to be not only savory to the taste but attractive to the eye. Just now the *architriclinus*—the chef—is beginning to prepare the carrots: he slices each piece lengthwise, then lengthwise again, to achieve slender, elongated triangles.

We look out across the river to the barbarian hosts, who in the slanting, gray light of winter mass like figures in a nightmare. Their hair (both of head and face) is uncut, vilely dressed with oil, braided into abhorrent shapes. Their bodies are distorted by ornament and discolored by paint. Some of the men are huge and muscular to the point of deformity, their legs wrapped comically in the garments called *braccae*—breeches. There is no discipline among them: they bellow at each other and race about in chaos. They are dirty, and they stink. A crone in a filthy blanket stirs a cauldron, slicing roots and bits of rancid meat into the concoction from time to time. She slices a carrot crosswise up its shaft, so that the circular pieces she cuts off float like foolish yellow eyes on the surface of her brew.

This unequal portrait of the two forces would not only have been the Roman view: it could almost have been the German view as well (for the milling hosts are of Germanic origin, as are all the intruders of this period). To the Romans, the German tribes were riffraff; to the Germans, the Roman side of the river was the place to be. The nearest we can come to understanding this divide may be the southern border of the United States. There the spit-and-polish troops are immigration police; the hordes, the Mexicans, Haitians, and other dispossessed peoples seeking illegal entry. The barbarian migration was not perceived as a threat by Romans, simply because it was a migration—a year-in, year-out, raggle-taggle migration—and not an organized, armed assault. It had, in fact, been going on for centuries. The Gauls had been the first barbarian invaders, hundreds of years before, and now Gaul lay at peace. The verses of its poets and the products of its vineyards were twin fountains of Roman inspiration. The Gauls had become more Roman than the Romans themselves. Why could not the same thing happen to these Vandals, Alans, and Sueves, now working themselves to a fever pitch on the far side of the river?

When, at last, the hapless Germans make their charge across the bridge of ice, it is head-on, without forethought or strategy. With preposterous courage they teem across the Rhine in convulsive waves, their principal weapon their own desperation. We get a sense of their numbers, as well as their desperation, in a single casualty count: the Vandals alone are thought to have lost twenty thousand *men* (not counting women and children) at the crossing. Despite their discipline, the Romans cannot hold back the Germanic sea.

From one perspective, at least, the Romans were overwhelmed by numbers—not just in this encounter but during centuries of migrations across the porous borders of the empire. Sometimes the barbarians came in waves, though seldom as big as this one. More often they came in trickles: as craftsmen who sought honest employment, as warriors who enlisted with the Roman legions, as tribal chieftains who paid for land, as marauders who burned and looted and sometimes raped and murdered.

What set them on the move was agriculture, which they had learned from their Roman neighbors. As the barbarian societies to the north of the empire turned from the nomadic ways of the hunter to the settled ways of the farmer, a seasonally predictable store of grain caused the inevitable population explosion. For all too obvious reasons, farmers live longer lives and see far more of their young reach adulthood than do hunters, whose precarious lives—and those of their progeny—are lived like an ecological high-wire act played without a net. For farmers, the safety net is the grain supply—more food than they need right now. This ancient form of money in the bank has served from time immemorial as the basis for long life, long-term planning, and all the arts of civilization.

But the complete formula is as invariable as it is archaic: economic success in the form of a store of grain triggers a

population explosion, which quickly triggers the need to ac-
quire new land to feed new mouths. Eleven centuries prior to
the encounter on the Rhine, an insignificant band of Latin-
speaking farmers "had but recently settled down to fixed agriculture and solved the problem of rapidly growing numbers by
embarking upon a career of conquest that ultimately eventuated
in the Roman empire," remarks the contemporary historian
William McNeill. "Considered in this light, the Roman state in
the West was destroyed by the same forces that had created it."

McNeill thus takes the sensible, need-based route of Machiavelli. But, as the classical historians have shown us, there are
other lights in which to consider this enormous transformation.
Why was the border guard so thin? Did the Romans not notice
—at some point—that their way of life was changing forever?
Did they not think to do something about it besides bow to the
inevitable? What *were* they thinking about? In order to answer
these questions and gain a fuller picture of Roman society, we
turn to a typical Roman who helped to build the world of late
antiquity.

The barbarian onslaught across the frozen Rhine occurred
in the first decade of the fifth century. Let us step back a
bit—into the fourth century—and meet a man whose style of
life can show us some of the yawning absences in Roman society, absences that would lead directly to the calamities of the
fifth century. He is Ausonius the poet, and he kept an impres-
sively large, exquisitely maintained country estate in Bordeaux
in the province of Gaul and, after his father's death, another
equally impressive estate in Aquitaine. Born just one hundred
years before the German migration over the Rhine, he was

raised not by his mother, of whom he doesn't seem to have had especially fond memories, but by two battle-axes, a grandmother and an aunt, both named Aemilia.

In his *Parentalia,* which might best be translated *Obsequies for the Forebears,* he extols their virtues. Of Grandmother Aemilia, he recalls:

> *et non deliciis ignoscere prompta pudendis*
> *ad perpendiculum seque suosque habuit.*
> To questionable pleasures she gave no quarter,
> but held both herself and her household rigidly upright.

The other Aemilia seems to have been rather large:

> *Aemilia, in cunis Hilari cognomen adepta,*
> *quod laeta et pueri comis ad effigiem,*
> *reddebas verum non dissimulanter ephebum.*
> Aemilia, nicknamed Lusty in your cradle,
> because you were as much fun as a boy—
> and, without trying, you always looked like a lad.

The rhetorical progression we are meant to notice here takes us through three stages of growth in three lines of poetry: infant *(in cunis);* boy *(pueri);* and adolescent *(ephebum).* Aemilia, though strapping, never grows quite as big as a man. Something, however, does keep growing in Aemilia.

Aunt Aemilia gets higher marks than Grandmother Aemilia, even if she must often have been severe toward the child Ausonius, who as a man designates her *virgo devota—* resolutely virginal—so resolute, in fact, that

feminei sexus odium tibi semper et inde
crevit devotae virginitatis amor.
hatred of the female sex forever grew within you
and from that sprang your love of consecrated maidenhood.

Though I am having some fun with this poetry, Ausonius is not. I am translating ambiguous lines to strengthen their ambiguity. Ausonius has surrounded these lines with conventional sentiments, no more fresh or interesting than what we might expect from a modern sympathy card. This, for instance, is how he ends the poem on his grandmother:

haec me praereptum cunis et ab ubere matris
blanda sub austeris inbuit inperiis.
tranquillos aviae cineres praestate, quieti
aeternum manes, si pia verba loquor.
By such kindnesses did she rear me—ripped from cradle
and mother's breast—but under the guise of stern
    commands.
Let my grandmother's ashes rest in peace,
ever silent shades, if I say the proper prayers.

Ausonius's friends might have been expected to notice that this is faint praise—but only because his praise indirectly draws attention to himself. Ah, dear Ausonius, they would have been expected to sigh, those women were hard on him, yet he remains so good, so loyal, fulfilling all the rites—*pia verba,* literally, faithful words—as is expected of him.

Ausonius's poetry is full of *pia verba;* except for the occasional, only half-intentional epiphanies (as in the poems about the Aemilias), there is little else. There are endless sequences about forebears, about former teachers, about daily life, about classical subjects (the heroes of the Trojan War, the Twelve Caesars), endless word games, and endless imitations of Virgil. He has one hot poem, "Cento Nuptualis," hot enough to be left untranslated in the Loeb *Ausonius,* where it has titillated as many generations of aging Latinists as it has frustrated generations of schoolboys—a clinical, cynical description of a bride's deflowering on her wedding night. Yet even here he is deliberately unoriginal: every phrase is taken from the poems of Virgil. Thus does he mean to avoid censure by appealing to the ultimate literary authority and to win admiration by a dazzling display of his knowledge of Virgil. But, apart from these *hommages,* there is almost never a memorable phrase, just high-class jingles, written to formula. His letters, also endless, are no better: there is seldom any necessary information to be communicated, insights are scarce, and genuine emotion is almost entirely absent. Though his effete contemporaries compared Ausonius to Virgil and Cicero, practically all others have found themselves in agreement with the robust opinion of Gibbon: "The poetical fame of Ausonius condemns the taste of his age."

How could a grown man have spent so much time so foolishly? Well, it's what everyone else was doing. This is a static world. Civilized life, like the cultivation of Ausonius's magnificent Bordeaux vineyards, lies in doing well what has been done before. Doing the expected is the highest value—and the second highest is like it: receiving the appropriate admiration of one's peers for doing it.

Though Ausonius is a Christian convert, as his "Oratio" shows, his Christianity is a cloak to be donned and removed, as needed. It was, no doubt, what everyone else was doing. His real worldview glimmers through all his work—a sort of agnostic paganism that enables him to evoke the silent shades of the pagan underworld without ever giving the reader the sense that he believes in any world but this one. In Ausonius—and all the other "best people" of the age, so like one another it is difficult to tell them apart—we see the flaw in Gibbon's analysis of Rome's fall. The vigorous gods of Rome were not eclipsed by some effeminate eastern fantasy religion. Fecund Venus and bloody Mars did not vacate the field to the pathetic, pacifist Christ. Rather, the life of the old religion had already drained away; and by the time Christianity came to the attention of the Roman gentry, the gods were shadows of their formerly lively selves—marginal, *quieti manes,* rustling through a dimly viewed eternity. It is no accident that when we today think of the Danube and the Rhine, the two rivers that divided the civilized world from the world of the northern barbarians, what come to mind are not the ghostly gods of Rome but the vigorous gods of the German tribes.

Ausonius made his career as a *grammaticus,* a professor of Latin, at Bordeaux, which then boasted one of the empire's great universities. His fame as a teacher reached even to the imperial court, and after thirty years in academe he was summoned to the Golden Palace in Milan (for the royal family no long resided at Rome) to become tutor to Gratian, son of Valentinian, emperor of the west. When in 368 Gratian was ordered to accompany his father on an anti-German campaign, Ausonius went along as a sort of poet laureate to the expedition, rising suitably to the occasion with his usual bland results —though this is also the period of the barracks humor of the "Cento Nuptualis," written, so Ausonius informs us, at the suggestion of the emperor himself. As one of his spoils of war,

Ausonius won the services of a German slave girl, whose charms he sang in his *Bissula* sequence:

Delicium, blanditiae, ludus, amor, voluptas,
barbara, sed quae Latias vincis alumna pupas.
Morsel—Blandishment—Sport—Desire—Climax—
Barbarian! but you, kid, are ahead of all the Latin girls.

It begins to sound like real poetry—with each noun alluding to the mounting tension of the poet's arousal till at the moment of orgasm *barbara* is moaned. But then you realize he's just aping Catullus.

In 375, the boy Gratian reached the throne, sharing it with his brother Valentinian II on the death of their father; and it is at this point that Ausonius's star enters its empyrean: he becomes *quaestor sacri palatii,* a sort of chief of staff to the emperors. In the same year, his aged father, pushing ninety, is named to the honorary post of prefect of Illyricum; in the next, his son is made proconsul of Africa. More honors tumble forth—for father, for son, for son-in-law, for nephew—and then in 379 Ausonius is named consul, the highest position any Roman (apart from the royal family) can attain.

In the old days of republican Rome, the consuls—there were two of them, so each could keep the other honest, elected for a term of one year to thus prevent dictatorship—had been the executive pinnacle of Roman government. But in the decisive sea battle of Actium in 31 B.C., Octavian had defeated his fellow consul Mark Antony, who had soiled republican virtue by lolling with Cleopatra in Egypt. Nobly seizing the imperial power, Octavian became Augustus Caesar, the first emperor—

and the consulships were henceforth transformed into honorary positions, vestigial reminders of republican virtue, and utterly ornamental.

The consulships were not the only ornamental offices in Roman society: the Eternal City was filled with the comings and goings of impotent men—senators, magistrates, bustling administrators of all kinds—performing meaningless duties. Augustus, while seizing all power, had wisely left in place all the republican trappings. The empty show that resulted only emphasized the more the importance of *how* things were done —since no one wished to advert to the vanity of *what* was being done. During the four centuries that elapsed from the time of Augustus to the time of Ausonius, the life of the capital turned ever more insubstantial and brittle, so that some ceremony or other, meticulously executed, could become the apogee of a man's life. In Ausonius's case the ceremony took the form of a convoluted oration, his *Gratiarum Actio,* or *Act of Thanksgiving,* given at the end of his consular year, in which he proffered incredibly elaborate and interminable thanks to the divine emperor's august presence.

The divine emperor's power rested, above all, in his office of *imperator,* commander in chief, the office whose importance had been so greatly expanded during the political upheavals of Augustus's day. But almost as important as his military power was his power to tax. "And it came to pass in those days," wrote Luke in the most famous passage on Roman taxation in all of literature, "that there went out a decree from Caesar Augustus, that all the world should be taxed." Thus is Jesus's birth set in the reign of the first emperor—*"toto orbe in pace composito"* ("all the world being at peace"), as a chronicler of the fifth century would soon describe it. But the peace of all the world—all the world worth thinking about, that is—came at a stiff price: the constant, and increasingly unequal, exactions of the emperor's tax men.

We know, again from the Gospels, the hatred of the Jews of the first century for the Roman tax collectors. By the time of Ausonius that hatred was universal. But now I must ask a great concession of my readers: to pity the poor tax man, whose life was far more miserable than the lives of those who suffered his exactions. The tax man, or *curialis,* was born that way: Can you imagine the dawning horror on realizing that you were born into a class of worms who were expected to spend their entire adult life spans collecting taxes from their immediate neighbors —and that there was no way out?

But this was only the beginning of the horror. Whatever the *curiales* were unable to collect they had to make good out of their own resources! Who were these wretches, and how were they assigned their doom? Since tax collection was patently beneath the dignity of the Ausonian class of great landowners, the task of collection fell to the next level down, to the small landowners, the squireens who had amassed just enough land to hold their heads up in polite society. Originally viewed as the first rung on the ladder of social betterment, the office of *curialis* had become by the age of Ausonius a cruel trap from which there was little chance of escape.

Of course, they tried to escape, especially during this period, as the tax base shrank and gold—the coin many taxes had to be paid in—rose in value against silver by about one percent a year. For a time, the wealthiest *curiales* succeeded in bribing their way onto the lists of senators, for the Senate was the cream of Roman society and the ancient, if ineffectual, symbol of its past republican glory—and senators paid no taxes. Others bribed their way out of their curial rank and into other ranks of the bureaucratic honeycomb, such as the enormous Palatine service. Some won commissions in the army; others sought refuge in priestly consecration. At the lowest end, *curiales* exchanged their birthrights to become members of a college of laborers, such as the grain importers and those engaged in river traffic. The most desperate—and as the century drew to its close these were becoming an ever larger plurality—borrowed from the only available lender, the lord of the local manor, whose class connections, as we can imply from the case of Ausonius, effectively exempted him from taxation. The lord was always happy to oblige: not only did he gain new relief from any shadow of taxation (for his debtor was both his tax assessor and his tax collector); in the end, after the *curialis* inevitably defaulted, his pleasant little farm would be added to the lord's expanding network of estates. Thus did the tax man often find himself a skilled but land-poor laborer, usually working for the local lord. Sometimes, the pitiable man and his family would sink so low as to become serfs on the land that once was theirs.

But the emperor had no intention of standing idly by while his tax collectors disappeared. He soon closed off all means of escape by legislating that *curiales* could not travel or sell their property without permission. Those in the Palatine service and the army were ordered back to their native stations. They could still become senators—providing they passed through all the grades of *curialis* and, on reaching the highest, *principalis,* remained in it for fifteen years. If anyone skipped a grade, he was —like a piece on a board game—to be returned to his starting point.

By the fifth century, in the years before the complete collapse of Roman government, the imperial approach to taxation had produced a caste as hopeless as any in history. Their rapacious exactions, taken wherever and whenever they could, were the direct result of their desperation about their own increasingly unpayable tax bills. As these nerved-up outcasts commenced to prey on whoever was weaker than they, the rich became even richer. The great landowners ate up the little ones, the tax base shrank still further, and the middle classes, never encouraged by the Roman state, began to disappear from the face of the earth. Nor would they return till the appearance of the Italian mercantile families of the high Middle Ages.

In the flight of the *curiales,* indeed, we hear the first faint notes of the medieval polity. As they, increasingly, swelled the ranks of the great lord's tenants, they were creating the fiefdoms of medieval Europe, complete with titled family, skilled artisans (or freemen), and serfs bound to the land. As the Germanic tribes poured over Gaul and Spain, and at last across the Italian peninsula, they settled down and took up farming like their Romanized neighbors. Their chiefs, too, became great lords of a kind, extending protection in return for labor and produce. To a fugitive tax collector, as to many another Roman on the run, the estate of a German chief could look considerably more attractive than that of his Roman counterpart. The German would welcome the fugitive's language, his connections, and his many civilized skills with rough enthusiasm—and the German would never have heard the word *curialis.* Thus did the great estates, gradually becoming laws unto themselves in a time of spreading civil chaos, grow slowly into the little kingdoms of the age of Charlemagne.

We should not think of the emperors as active persecutors of the poor *curiales.* (They actually thought of themselves as protecting them—and all Roman citizens—from the cruel vagaries of life beyond the Roman *orbis*. And, after all, what blessedness could be greater than the honor of Roman citizenship? An imperial edict of this period even tries to shame the recusant *curiales* by reminding them of their noble rank, of "the splendor of their birth.") Rather, the bureaucratic and social establishments of Rome had become so top-heavy and entrenched that effective reform was no longer possible. Class was insulated from class. We cannot imagine Ausonius, for instance, giving a thought to the sufferings of any but his own. The *passio curialis,* had it ever crossed his mind, would only have prompted another clever little poem for his friends to chuckle at. In Ausonius we encounter the complete extinction of *Res Publica,* the Public Thing—social concern. In all his extant corpus, there is but one appearance by a person not of Ausonius's class—Bissula, the German slave girl with the funny name, who is there only to prop up Ausonius's manhood.

The emperor's worst headache was the army itself. Starved for taxes, he was unable to maintain a force that could withstand the ever-strengthening barbarian onslaughts. But since the time of Constantine, new emperors had come from the army—or at least been approved by the army—so that the existence of the army was a veiled threat to every reigning emperor. The army had made emperors and pulled them from their throne—and one was hard put to recall an emperor who had lasted more than a few years or had died in his bed. In 383 the army in Britain mutinied and, under the leadership of Maximus, crossed to the continent and began to occupy Gaulish cities. Young Gratian was assassinated at Lyons and his brother driven from Italy. Ausonius's career was over. By the time order was restored under a new emperor—Theodosius in 388—Ausonius was too old for public life.

Though it is difficult to imagine the Pax Romana lasting as long as it did without the increasing militarization of the Imperium Romanum, the Romans themselves were never happy about their army. It suggested dictatorship, rather than those good old republican values, and they preferred to avert their eyes, keeping themselves carefully ignorant of the army's essential contribution to their well-being. With the moral decay of republican resolve, the army became more and more a reserve of non-Romans, half-Romanized barbarian mercenaries and servants sent in the stead of freemen who couldn't be bothered. In the last days of the empire, men commonly mutilated themselves to escape service, though such a crime was—in theory—punishable by torture and death. Military levies, sent to the great estates, met such resistance that influential landowners were allowed to send money, instead of men, to the army. In 409, faced with an increasingly undefended frontier, the emperor announced the impossible: henceforth, slaves would be permitted, even encouraged, to enlist, and for their service they would receive a bounty and their freedom. By this point, it was sometimes difficult to tell the Romans from the barbarians—at least along the frontier.

There are, no doubt, lessons here for the contemporary reader. The changing character of the native population, brought about through unremarked pressures on porous borders; the creation of an increasingly unwieldy and rigid bureaucracy, whose own survival becomes its overriding goal; the despising of the military and the avoidance of its service by established families, while its offices present unprecedented opportunity for marginal men to whom its ranks had once been closed; the lip service paid to values long dead; the pretense that we still are what we once were; the increasing concentrations of the populace into richer and poorer by way of a corrupt tax system, and the desperation that inevitably follows; the aggrandizement of executive power at the expense of the legislature; ineffectual legislation promulgated with great show; the moral vocation of the man at the top to maintain order at all costs, while growing blind to the cruel dilemmas of ordinary life—these are all themes with which our world is familiar, nor are they the God-given property of any party or political point of view, even though we often act as if they were. At least, the emperor could not heap his economic burdens on posterity by creating long-term public debt, for floating capital had not yet been conceptualized. The only kinds of wealth worth speaking of were the fruits of the earth.

Though it is easy for us to perceive the wild instability of the Roman Imperium in its final days, it was not easy for the Romans. Rome, the Eternal City, had been untouchable since the Celts of Gaul had sacked it by surprise in 390 B.C. In the ensuing eight centuries Rome built itself into the world's only superpower, unassailable save for the occasional war on a distant border. The Gauls had long since become civilized Romans, and Rome offered the same Romanization to anyone who wanted it—sometimes, as with the Jews, whether they wanted it or not. Normally, though, everyone was dying to be Roman. As Theodoric, the homely king of the Ostrogoths, was fond of saying: "An able Goth wants to be like a Roman; only a poor Roman would want to be like a Goth."

The citizens of the City of Rome, therefore, could not believe it when toward the end of the first decade of the fifth century, they woke to find Alaric, king of the Visigoths, and all his forces parked at their gates. He might as well have been the king of the Fuzzy-Wuzzies, or any other of the inconsequential outlanders that civilized people have looked down their noses at throughout history. It was preposterous. They dispatched a pair of envoys to conduct the tiresome negotiation and send him away. The envoys began with empty threats: any attack on Rome was doomed, for it would be met by invincible strength and innumerable ranks of warriors. Alaric was a sharp man, and in his rough fashion a just one. He also had a sense of humor.

"The thicker the grass, the more easily scythed," he replied evenly.

The envoys quickly recognized that their man was no fool. All right, then, what was the price of his departure? Alaric told them: his men would sweep through the city, taking all gold, all silver, and everything of value that could be moved. They would also round up and cart off every barbarian slave.

But, protested the hysterical envoys, what will that leave us?

Alaric paused. "Your lives."

In that pause, Roman security died and a new world was conceived.

II

What
Was Lost

*The Complexities of
the Classical Tradition*

So they kept their lives, most of them. But sooner or later they or their progeny lost almost everything else: titles, property, way of life, learning—especially learning. A world in chaos is not a world in which books are copied and libraries maintained. It is not a world where learned men have the leisure to become more learned. It is not a world for which the *grammaticus* schedules regular classes of young scholars and knowledge is dutifully transmitted year by placid year.

Between the Sack of Rome by Alaric in 410 and the death of the last western emperor in 476, the Imperium became increasingly unstable. The large landowners—more and more, laws unto themselves—ignored the emperor's decrees, going even so far as to use the great public edifices as quarries for private palaces. Rome itself, abandoned by the emperors for the more defensible marshes of Ravenna, saw the splendor of its public buildings crumble before the destructiveness of private greed. Though the emperor announced dire punishments for any official who cooperated in this destruction—fifty pounds of gold for a magistrate, a flogging and the loss of both hands for a subordinate—the looting continued unabated. The Vandals were not the only vandals.

The straight Roman road, solidly paved, unwilling to compromise with the vagaries of local landscape, and for centuries the symbol of safe and unmolested travel, now presented the likelihood of unwelcome adventure. Not only were there bands of highway robbers, increasingly composed of the ruined and the dispossessed; the emperor's own *curiosi* (a combination of highway police and customs guards) began to extort bribes from travelers desperate to reach places of greater safety, often halting the wayfarers' progress when they had no more bribes to proffer. Throughout the countryside, once the very image of Roman peace, illegal brotherhoods of extortionists formed —the proto-Mafiosi. *Curiales* and other struggling middle-class townsmen, who had been accustomed to sending their infants to be nursed by shepherds in pure mountain air, began to find it impossible to retrieve those children. Snatched away to inaccessible mountain fastnesses, the children were raised brutally as shepherd-slaves, and the name *shepherd* became synonymous with thief, kidnapper, trafficker in children. The fear of such kidnapping still finds echoes in the lost children and loathsome adults who haunt the deep wood of European fairy tales.

As barbarian attacks became not a distant possibility but the order of the day, records of ownership and purchase were often lost in raids, thus presenting a fine opportunity to the emperor's *discussores* (the super-*curiales*). These rapacious bullies would descend with a large retinue on a recently looted farm, demanding of the disoriented owner that he render all accounts forthwith. What would follow, as described in the emperor's own reform-minded, if ineffectual, edict, is enough to curl one's hair— *"innumerae deinde caedes, saeva custodia, suspendiorum crudelitas, et universa tormenta"* ("thence innumerable slaughters, savage imprisonment, the cruelty of hangings, and every kind of torture").

The borders of the empire were contracting. By the end of the third decade of the fifth century, the grain-heavy plain of northern Africa—Rome's breadbasket—was lost to the Vandals, who had already seized or savaged large swaths of Spain and Gaul. Through most of the century, various armies of Goths, then of Huns, driving westward over the Danube and decimating the eastern provinces, marched up and down the Italian peninsula, raising panic and leaving desolation. As the fifth century opened, the Roman garrison in Britain was already on its way to depletion, so desperately were soldiers needed elsewhere. By 410, the year of Alaric's Sack, it had been withdrawn completely, exposing Britain more than ever to the depredations of the Germanic Angles and Saxons on its eastern shore and to the even more terrifying slave raids of the Celts of Ireland along its jagged western bays.

One of the most horrifying features of the period is the wholesale enslavement of freemen and -women. Estate agents for the great landlords often acted as *redemptores,* redeemers of Roman citizens seized in barbarian raids. The object was usually not the freedom of the Roman prisoner, but his fresh enslavement as a serf on the landlord's estate. The ransom paid was a cheap price for a lifetime of service from the liberated prisoner. Sometimes the ruse was even simpler: at the time of an invasion, a local farmer would be given shelter for himself and his family on a great estate, only to find that, when the barbarian hordes had passed, neither he nor his would ever be free to leave.

The barbarians, too, were likely to enslave whomever they could lay their hands on. In the slavery business, no tribe was fiercer or more feared than the Irish. They were excellent sailors—in skin-covered craft that they maneuvered with consummate skill. Just before dawn, a small war party would move its stealthy oval coracles into a little cove, approach an isolated farmhouse with silent strides, grab some sleeping children, and be halfway back to Ireland before anyone knew what had happened.

The Irish moved in larger war parties, as well. One day in

401 or thereabouts, a great fleet of black coracles swept up the west coast of Britain, probably into the Severn estuary, and, seizing (according to an eyewitness) "many thousands" of young prisoners, returned with them to a slave market in Ireland. We still have the testimony of one of the captives, a boy of sixteen who called himself Patricius. He tells us that his father, Calpurnius, was (God help him) a *curialis* and that his grandfather Potitus had been a Catholic priest—so he was a middle-class lad, a Romanized Briton looking forward to a classical education and a career. Not surprisingly, he was not interested in following in his father's footsteps: "I sold my noble rank, I blush not to state it nor am I sorry." Whatever the plans of this brash young man, they were cut short by the terrible Irish raid. He finds himself "chastened exceedingly and humbled in truth by hunger and nakedness and that daily," as a shepherd-slave in the Irish district of Antrim, as the property of a local "king" named Miliucc. What became of Patricius will form the subject of a later chapter, after we have left the civilized world for good and journeyed to the unholy land of Ireland.

But before we bid goodnight to the late classical world and make our way to the fiercest of the fierce barbarians, we must consider one last question: What was lost when the Roman Empire fell? The life of Ausonius can show us the why of the Fall, but it gives us nothing to weep for. Classical civilization— the world that came to birth in the Athens of Pericles five centuries before Christ and that dies now five hundred years after Christ in the century of the barbarian invasions—is worth a far better elegy than Ausonius can provide. What died, when no one any longer had the leisure to pass on the essentials of the classical tradition, when the barbarians burned the libraries and the books turned to dust, when the stones remaining were reassembled into rural outhouses?

We find the answer in the life of Augustine of Hippo, almost the last great classical man—and very nearly the first medieval man.

J ust thirty years before Patricius was brought in chains to Ireland, another teenager with a similar background—a Romanized African whose father was a petty official—came all too willingly, not to an impossible hinterland, but to the seething capital of Roman Africa. "To Carthage I came," recalled Augustine later, "where there sang all around me in my ears a cauldron of unholy loves. As yet I loved no one, yet I loved to love, and out of a deep-seated need, I hated myself for not being needy. I pursued whoever-whatever might be lovable, in love with love. Safety I hated—and any course without danger. For within me was a famine."

This is clear, poignant, ruthless prose. But though it still reads awfully well, the words of Augustine's *Confessions* no longer jump with the fresh shock they held when he published his memoir in 401—probably the same year Patricius was kidnapped. The reason for this is that Augustine's is a sensibility that has since become so common that we no longer experience the *Confessions* as the earthquake they were felt to be by readers of late antiquity. For Augustine is the first human being to say "I"—and to mean what we mean today. His *Confessions* are, therefore, the first genuine autobiography in human history. The implications of this are staggering and, even today, difficult to encompass. A good start is made, of course, by reading the *Confessions* themselves and falling under their spell. But in order to grasp the enormity of Augustine's achievement, one must read the "autobiographies" that went before him.

Open any collection of Great Thoughts or Great Sayings— especially one that, like *Bartlett's,* goes in chronological order— and let your eye pick out the *I*'s. In the oldest literature their paucity and lack of force will begin to impress you. Of course, characters in Homer refer to themselves occasionally as "I." Socrates even speaks of his *daimon,* his inner spirit. But personal revelation, such as we are utterly accustomed to, is nowhere to be found. Even lyric poems tend to be objective by our standards, and the exceptions stand out: a fragment ("The moon has set . . ."),✤ attributed to Sappho, and the Psalms, attributed to King David.

When in the classical period we reach the first works to be designated as autobiographies, we can only be confounded by their impersonal tone. Marcus Aurelius, by Gibbon's standards the most enlightened emperor and the great philosopher of Roman antiquity, speaks to us in epigrams, like Confucius and Ecclesiastes before him: "This Being of mine, whatever it really is, consists of a little flesh, a little breath, and the part which governs"—he means his mind. This is as confidential as Marcus gets. Or how about this for a personal revelation? "All that is harmony for you, my Universe, is in harmony with me as well. Nothing that comes at the right time for you is too early or too late for me." For all their ponderousness, the great emperor's thoughts are never more personal than a Chinese fortune cookie.

✤ The moon has set
and the Pleiades:
it is the middle of the night,
and time passes, yes passes—
and I lie alone.

Then we reach Augustine, who tells us everything—his jealousies in infancy, his thieving as a boy, his stormy relationship with his overbearing mother (the ever-certain Monica), his years of philandering, his breakdowns, his shameful love for an unnamed peasant woman, whom he finally sends away. His self-loathing is as modern as that of a character in Camus or Beckett—and as concrete: "I carried inside me a cut and bleeding soul, and how to get rid of it I just didn't know. I sought every pleasure—the countryside, sports, fooling around, the peace of a garden, friends and good company, sex, reading. My soul floundered in the void—and came back upon me. For where could my heart flee from my heart? Where could I escape from myself?"

No one had ever talked this way before. If we page quickly through world literature from its beginnings to the advent of Augustine, we realize that with Augustine human consciousness takes a quantum leap forward—and becomes self-consciousness. Here for the first time is a man consistently observing himself not as Man but as this singular man—Augustine. From this point on, true autobiography becomes possible, and so does its near relative, subjective and autobiographical fiction. Fiction had always been there, in the form of storytelling. But now for the first time there glimmers the possibility of psychological fiction: the subjective story, the story of a soul. Though the cry of Augustine—the Man Who Cried "I"—will seldom be heard again in full force until the early modern period, he is the father not only of autobiography but of the modern novel. He is also a distinguished forebear of the modern science of psychology.

hat prepared Augustine to be Augustine? What was the ground, and what the seed?

Augustine was among the last of classically educated men. Born in 354 into what all believed to be a stable world, he would witness in old age—in the 420s—the last days of the *grammaticus*. His Latin has a refinement and a piquancy that few could match in any period of antiquity. The delicate changes rung on three words—*love, need, hate*—in the famous passage from the *Confessions* quoted above mark him as adhering to the highest standards of classical rhetoric. What Ausonius wore like a medal Augustine bears stamped on his heart: the show-off accomplishments of Ausonius are for Augustine honored disciplines of the spirit.

Augustine gives us the world's first description of how a child may fall hopelessly in love with literature—a fall so palpable it is almost carnal. Like creative children in every age, he despised his first school assignments in "reading, writing, and arithmetic" because they were nothing but rote: " 'One and one are two; two and two are four'—what hateful singsong." Nor did he like any better his first lessons in Greek, accompanied by the teacher's "punishments and cruel threats"; and he states succinctly the complaint of numberless generations of students before and after him: "Mastering a foreign language was as bitter as gall, for not one word of it did I understand." But then, after all the dreary classes of grinding recitation, he is handed real literature in his own tongue: "I loved Latin . . . and I wept for Dido slain, she 'seeking by the sword a stroke and wound extreme.' "

Despairing Dido, queen of ancient Carthage, slain by her

own hand as her magnificent lover Aeneas lifts anchor and sails away forever: this is one of the most haunting and permanent images of the classical world. What opened Augustine's heart to Latin literature was Virgil's *Aeneid, the* literary masterpiece of the Roman world, its Bible and its Shakespeare in one. The *Aeneid* is a conscious literary epic, not a folk epic like the Greek *Iliad.* Picking up where Homer leaves off—with the fall of Troy to the Greek forces, who penetrate its impregnable walls by the "gift" of a huge hollow horse lined with armed men—Virgil recounts the exploits of his hero, Aeneas, son of Venus and a Trojan father. *"Arma virumque cano"* ("I sing of arms and the man"), begins Virgil in a great trumpet fanfare. As all Virgil's readers could savor with thrilling foreknowledge, Aeneas will miraculously escape the certain doom of burning Troy, faithfully carrying his ancient father on his back and holding his little son by the hand. A wanderer, he is received with high celebration by the queen of Carthage, who is riveted by his tale. Dido and Aeneas are fated to fall passionately in love, but Aeneas always knows—as does the reader—that, though it will break Dido's heart and end her life, he must move bravely on to his destiny, the founding of the City of Rome.

Virgil wrote in the age of Caesar Augustus, the first emperor, and he conceived the *Aeneid* as a national epic (the only completely successful one in world literature), orchestrated artfully to evoke in the reader a wave of patriotism for the great empire's heroic beginnings. This younger, less seasoned civilization of the Latin west, having absorbed, both politically and culturally, the lofty civilization of the Greek east, needed to establish its own legitimacy to rule and to overwhelm. To the Greeks, the Romans were cocky and underbred. To the Romans, the Greeks were too clever by half—and more than a little unsavory. (In observing a refined Hellene flaunt his superiority, your regular, plainspoken Roman could not help but let the suspicion of perversion play at the back of his mind: by Jupiter, don't they look the other way and let those faggoty tutors they hire bugger their own children?) The cultural relation of Roman to Greek was, in many ways, not unlike the cultural relation of Englishman to Frenchman and of American to Englishman: in all three relations, simplicity is the virtue and complexity the vice on one side, while on the other subtlety is prized and (supposedly rustic) straightforwardness can give offense.

In Virgil's new myth, forthright Rome is the moral superior of sneaky Greece and (surprise!) actually the older civilization, since it can trace its roots to fabled Ilium—ancient Troy. Virgil makes his new myth unforgettable by framing it in a new language that rivals anything Greece ever produced: a heroic but flexible Latin that still rings down the ages. In recounting the story of the hollow horse, by which the Greeks won through duplicity what they could not win fair and square on the field of battle, Aeneas warns not only Dido but all of subsequent humanity: *"Timeo Danaos et dona ferentis"* ("I am wary of Greeks, even bearing gifts").

In Dido there is more than a hint of another dusky African queen—the Cleopatra whose "eastern" sensuality did in Mark Antony. But our hero Aeneas is virtuous enough, in the end, to reject even this temptation against his—and every Roman's—destiny. Of course, he is flesh and blood, and no prig either, and the lovemaking of these two is the occasion for some of Virgil's most exciting poetry. But Dido's suicide, though genuine tragedy, is necessary. This is—for Greeks as well as Romans—the ancient meaning of tragedy: unavoidable catastrophe.

And it is to Dido, especially, that we may apply the greatest of all Virgil's great lines:

Sunt lacrimae rerum et mentem mortalia tangunt.
These are the tears of things,
    and the stuff of our mortality cuts us to the heart.

To Augustine, provincial Roman of Africa born, Dido was less exotic than she would have appeared to an Italian; she was, in some respects, an incarnation of Africa, and her catastrophe was Africa's catastrophe: sensuous Africa, whose great City of Carthage was Dido's city . . . and was now, from his lascivious seventeenth year, Augustine's city—the city that boiled without while Augustine boiled within.

The famous sentence "To Carthage I came . . ." contains a purposeful rhyme, one of the first in Latin literature.[*] The city's name, *Carthago,* rhymes with *sartago,* cauldron. This is incantatory, meant to draw our attention to the bubbling of the city and the bubbling of the boy, macrocosm and microcosm. A powerful and subtle rhetorical device, it would nonetheless have been eschewed by all earlier writers as *indecens*—rustic and inappropriate. But, unlike the *déraciné* Ausonius, Augustine, the budding African Latinist who could identify so completely with Dido's passion, can allow his inner bubbling to surface from time to time in the form of African rhythms and rhetorical devices. After his conversion and consecration as bishop of

[*] I think it is the second. The first I find is in Jerome's Latin translation of Paul's letter to Titus: *"Bonum certamen certavi, cursum consumavi, fidem servavi"* ("I have fought the good fight, I have finished the race, I have kept my word"). But, rather than being deliberate, this rhyme may have appeared simply unavoidable to Jerome.

Hippo, Augustine will repeatedly delight his congregations by employing verbal pyrotechnics with an African "swing." *"Bona dona"* ("Good gifts") will become one of their favorites. In this vernacularizing of Latin, we may discern the first step toward the simplified, rhythmic, rhyming "people's Latin" of the Middle Ages.

If Virgil was the great teacher of language and style (or grammar and rhetoric, to use the categories of the medieval school), Cicero was the great teacher of argument or disputation (dialectic, to use the medieval term). As Virgil's Greek counterpart was—very roughly speaking—Homer, so Cicero's Greek counterpart was Demosthenes. The two dialecticians have cast their shadows over the otherwise happy schooldays of countless students of the Greek and Latin classics. The boy C. S. Lewis, deliriously satisfied while basking in the high sun of Homer's war stories and in the soft afternoon of the discreetly erotic Catullus and the discreetly precise Tacitus, at last confronts the approaching gloom: "The Two Great Bores (Demosthenes and Cicero) could not be avoided."

Homer and Virgil are art, and each was to his age and place what good movies are to ours—never a chore, always refreshing, occasionally ennobling. Demosthenes and Cicero are hard work, and were studied in Augustine's day as paragons of the "art" of persuasion—the kind of thing one might study today in journalism school. If the *Aeneid* is language as metaphor, as the sacramental ritualizing of human experience, Cicero's speeches are language as practical tool. A two-thousand-year-old poem may still, conceivably, speak to us with as much force as it did to the people of its day. We would not expect the same from a two-thousand-year-old newspaper editorial or a two-thousand-year-old advertising jingle. Nor should we expect it from Cicero.

Cicero, born in the century before Christ, exercised his techniques when republican Rome, in all its vigor, welcomed public men. Augustine loved Cicero, as did the whole Latin world, which placed the Roman orator just below Virgil on the divinity charts. (Jerome, the cantankerous translator of the Latin Bible, awoke one night in a frenzied sweat: he had dreamed that Christ had condemned him to hell for being more a Ciceronian than a Christian.) The ancients held the practical use of words in much higher regard than we do, probably because they were much closer to the oral customs of prehistoric village life—so clearly reflected in Nestor's speech to the Greek chieftains in the *Iliad* and in Mark Antony's speech over Julius Caesar's body—in which the fate of an entire race may hang on one man's words.

But we are made uncomfortable and bored by Cicero's elaborately coaching us in all the tricks of his trade—the many techniques for convincing others to act the way we want them to. For Cicero, "to speak from the heart" would be the rashest foolishness; one must always speak from calculation: What do I want to see happen here? What are the desires of my audience? How can I motivate them to do my will? How shall I disguise my weakest arguments? How dazzle my listeners so they are no longer able to reason matters through independently?

The techniques of the successful politician, the methods of modern advertising—the whole panoply of persuasion is to be found in Cicero. The figure closest to him in our own age might be Dale Carnegie, who advised that every single word and gesture be calculated to "win" and "influence." However squeamish such advice may make us, to the ancients it made perfect sense. For in addition to learning how to write a poem for one's own satisfaction, in addition to learning how to turn a phrase in a letter so as to please a friend, there was a larger literary task to be played out in the larger world—the *polis*—to which all educated men were bound to make their contribution, to bring their positive influence to bear. And this world of politics required the arts of persuasion, if one were to meet with success. In Ausonius, classical education calcified into the merely ornamental. In Augustine, it remains as vigorous as it had been in Cicero's day, and Augustine will spend his life using Cicero's elaborate and nuanced arsenal of techniques on behalf of a new worldview and a new political agenda. This will be the public contribution of Augustine, the Roman citizen, to the dying Roman *Res Publica*.

Besides the arts of rhetoric and persuasion, there was a third pursuit for the liberally educated man, a pursuit only a gifted seeker could successfully embark on: the way of philosophy. Beyond the literary arts lies, however dimly perceived, the Ascent to Truth, to Wisdom. In Augustine's day, this ascent was illumined by the works of one great teacher: Plato, the Greek philosopher who had been Socrates's pupil and who was born in the time and place that all educated men looked to as the Golden Age—Athens in the fifth century B.C.

If the liberal arts were for the few, philosophy was for the fewer. Many liberally educated men did not even assent to the goal of philosophy, because they did not think it possible to attain to Truth or Wisdom with any certitude. Cicero was such an agnostic: after a long pursuit of philosophical truth, he found himself siding with the Skeptics, who believed in the uncertainty of all ultimate knowledge (though he inclined in moral matters to the school of the Stoics, who believed with certitude that virtue will yield happiness). Cicero's even-tempered agnosticism will come as no surprise to anyone in our world who has noticed what a convenient philosophy it makes for Cicero's contemporary children: publicists, marketeers, and all those who seek to motivate us to do what we might otherwise not think to do. As a philosopher, Cicero was the great packager of his age, an unoriginal thinker with real flair, a sort of Will Durant, who could dramatize all the currents and schools of thought so that anyone might understand them well enough to talk about them at a cocktail party.

But Augustine wanted Truth, not cheap success: such a pressure-cooker psyche can settle for nothing less. He soon abandoned the simple, emotional Catholicism of his mother and adopted something more exclusive and *récherché:* the religion of Mani, a Persian syncretist who had taken this and that from here and there and come up with something that can only strike us as a California cult—a little Christian symbolism, a large dose of Zoroastrian dualism, and some of the quiet refinements of Buddhism. It was called Manicheism. For a while, it let Augustine off the hook. For one thing, it absolved him from any responsibility for his raging lusts: in Mani's system, Good was passive, unable to battle the gross and fleshly evils that raged against it. It was a made-to-order religion for a smart young provincial who needed to explore every dark corner of the boiling city and experience every dark pleasure it had to offer —and at the same time think himself above the herd. But it couldn't keep up with Augustine's fearlessly inquiring mind. Like Jehovah's Witnesses or Mormonism, it was full of assertions, but could yield no intellectual system to nourish a great intellect.

We don't know what Augustine read, but we know he devoured books. By his own admission, he never learned Greek properly. Plato, however, was readily available in translation—and "packaged" by commentators of far greater profundity than Cicero. Plato was in the air Augustine breathed, the figure a thoughtful young man must sooner or later test himself against.

Augustine, disappointed with Manicheism and now appointed to his first big job as professor of rhetoric at Milan, forms a new—and, of course, exclusive—group: a temporary "monastic" community of like-minded young men who mean to ascend to Truth with the aid of Plato and his Latin commentators. Their earnest intentions will eventually be thwarted when their wives-to-be object to all this moping about. And, soon enough, Augustine's mother will arrive on the scene, creating, as she always does, emotional tornadoes and hurricanes—a sort of one-woman African Sturm und Drang. But the establishment, even for a short time, of such a community gives us an idea of how seriously and personally the pursuit of philosophy could be taken in the ancient world—something far closer to an ashram than to a modern department of philosophy. And this community will provide Augustine with the seedbed he needs for his own philosophy to germinate.

Socrates, at least in Plato's accounts of him, did not so much build a positive philosophy as pose questions, questions that show up the utter foolishness of his interlocutors' assumptions. He, of course, invented the Socratic method, forcing his students to start their quest for Truth with a confession of their own ignorance. Plato, the product of this method, reasons with delicate skill toward the creation of a large and airy edifice—the grandest construct of ancient philosophy.

Plato begins with his own experience of a spark of divinity in all the creatures of the natural world, a spark he experiences particularly in himself and other human beings—in other words, the *daimon* of Socrates. But the spark is experienced within a world of corruption and death, the world of the flesh. It is worth our while to take a few moments to receive Plato in his own words, for they give us an idea both of the challenge confronting Augustine and of the flavor of the Augustinian ashram. (Most of Plato is impenetrable on first reading. If it begins to give you a headache, skip to the end of the passage— and just take my word for it.) Here is Plato in the *Phaedrus* on the spark, the *daimon*—the soul:

Of the nature of the soul [*psyche* in Greek], though her true form be ever a theme of large and more than mortal discourse, let me speak briefly and in a figure. And let the figure be composite—a pair of winged horses and a charioteer. Now the winged horses and the charioteers of the gods are all of them noble and of noble descent, but those of other races are mixed; the human charioteer drives his in a pair; and one of them is noble and of noble breed, and the other is ignoble and of ignoble breed; and the driving of them of necessity gives a great deal of trouble to him. I will endeavor to explain to you in what way the mortal differs from the immortal creature. The soul in her totality has the care of inanimate being everywhere, and traverses the whole heaven in divers forms appearing: —when perfect and fully winged she soars upward, and orders the whole world; whereas the imperfect soul, losing her wings and drooping in her flight at last settles on the solid ground—there, finding a home, she receives an earthly frame which appears to be self-moved, but is really moved by her power; and this composition of soul and body is called a living and mortal creature. For immortal no such union can be reasonably believed to be; although fancy, not having seen nor surely known the nature of God, may imagine an immortal creature having both a body and also a soul which are united throughout all time. Let that, however, be as God wills, and be spoken of acceptably to him. And now let us ask the reason why the soul loses her wings!

The wing is the corporeal element which is most akin to the divine, and which by nature tends to soar aloft and carry that which gravitates downwards into the upper region, which is the habitation of the gods. The divine is beauty, wisdom, goodness, and the like; and by these the wing of the soul is nourished, and grows apace; but when fed upon evil and foulness and the opposite of good, wastes and falls away. Zeus, the mighty lord, holding the reins of a winged chariot, leads the way to heaven, ordering all and taking care of all; and there follows him the array of gods and demigods, marshalled in eleven bands; Hestia alone abides at home in the house of heaven; of the rest they who are reckoned among the princely twelve march in their appointed order. They see many blessed sights in the inner heaven, and there are many ways to and fro, along which the blessed gods are passing, everyone doing his own work; he may follow who will and can, for jealousy has no place in the celestial choir. But when they go to banquet and festival, then they move up the steep to the top of the vault of heaven. The chariots of the gods in even poise, obeying the rein, glide happily; but the others labour, for the vicious steed goes heavily, weighing down the charioteer to the earth when his steed has not been thoroughly trained:—and this is the hour of agony and extremest conflict for the soul. For the immortals, when they are at the end of their course, go forth and stand upon the outside of heaven, and the revolution of the spheres carries them round, and they behold the things beyond. But of the heaven which is above the heavens, what earthly poet ever did or ever will sing worthily? It is such as I will describe; for I must dare to speak the truth, when truth is my theme. There abides the very being with which true knowledge is concerned; the colorless, formless, intangible essence, visible only to mind, the pilot of the soul. The divine intelligence, being nurtured upon mind and pure knowledge, and the intelligence of every soul which is capable of receiving the food proper to it, rejoices at beholding reality, and once more gazing upon truth, is replenished and made glad, until the revolution of the worlds brings her round again to the same place. In the revolution she beholds justice, and temperance, and knowledge absolute, not in the form of generation or of relation, which men call existence, but knowledge absolute in existence absolute; and beholding the other true existences in like manner, and feasting upon them, she passes down into the interior of the heavens and returns home; and there the charioteer putting up his horses at the stall, gives them ambrosia to eat and nectar to drink.

Such is the life of the gods; but of other souls, that which follows God best and is likest to him lifts the head of the charioteer into the outer world, and is carried round in the revolution, troubled indeed by the steeds, and with difficulty beholding true being; while another only rises and falls, and sees, and again fails to see by reason of the unruliness of the steeds. The rest of the souls are also longing after the upper world and they all follow, but not being strong enough they are carried round below the surface, plunging, treading on one another, each striving to be first; and there is confusion and perspiration and the extremity of effort; and many of them are lamed or have their wings broken through the ill-driving of the charioteers; and all of them after a fruitless toil, not having attained to the mysteries of true being, go away, and feed upon opinion. The reason why the souls exhibit this exceeding eagerness to behold the plain of truth is that pasturage is found there, which is suited to the highest part of the soul; and the wing on which the soul soars is nourished with this. And there is a law of Destiny, that the soul which attains any vision of truth in company with a god is preserved from harm until the next period, and if attaining always is always unharmed. But when she is unable to follow, and fails to behold the truth, and through some ill-hap sinks beneath the double load of forgetfulness and vice, and her wings fall from her and she drops to the ground, then the law ordains that this soul shall at her first birth pass, not into any other animal, but only into man; and the soul which has seen most of truth shall come to the birth as a philosopher, or artist, or some musical and loving nature; that which has seen truth in the second degree shall be some righteous king or warrior chief; the soul which is of the third class shall be a politician, or economist, or trader; the fourth shall be a lover of gym-

nastic toils, or a physician; the fifth shall lead the life of a
prophet or hierophant; to the sixth the character of a poet
or some other imitative artist will be assigned; to the seventh the life of an artisan or husbandman; to the eighth
that of a sophist or demagogue; to the ninth that of a
tyrant;—all these are states of probation, in which he who
does righteously improves, and he who does unrigh-
teously deteriorates his lot.

Plato is the greatest of all Greek prose stylists, and through
his tightly woven sentences run threads of delicate beauty and
allusive grace. He doesn't sound like anyone else; and he convinces us not only of the largeness of his mind, but of the
genuine mysticism of his spirit. He tells us from the start that he
is using metaphor, but we cannot help believe that he has
glimpsed the world beyond the veil. He has at least as much in
common with the wisdom of the east—with Buddhism and
Taoism—as he does with the subsequent philosophy of the
west. He is simply the great philosopher, and the difficulty one
experiences in understanding him is not a difficulty based on
superficial obfuscation but on his genuine profundity. No one
grasps Plato by reading him through quickly or once.

So it was for Augustine, and thus the necessity of the
ashram and stillness and philosophical companionship. Augustine's spirit resonates with the plangent chords of Plato: the
restless, exiled soul, looking everywhere for its true home,
feasting on sewage while dimly remembering the nectar and
ambrosia of high heaven. Plato is right, and his are the most
profound descriptions in all the ancient world of the miraculous
golden flashes of yearning embedded in the dross of reality—
the out-of-jointness of the universe. Who else, Augustine asks

himself, even talks of these things? And then the answer comes to him: Saul of Tarsus, the wiry, bald-headed Jew whose awkward, importunate letters, signed "Paul," the Christians have been using as scripture: "For the flesh lusteth against the Spirit, and the Spirit against the flesh: and these are contrary the one to the other: so that ye cannot do the things that ye would."

Surely this is meaningless coincidence: what could a sweaty little nobody, dashing about the Mediterranean basin, have in common with the loftiest philosopher of all? And yet . . . Augustine begins to read Paul seriously. He entertains the possibility that Plato even has something wrong—that the ascent to Truth is not a task the philosopher takes upon himself and succeeds at by his own effort. Has the great Plato mistakenly equated knowledge with virtue? For if the flesh and the spirit are at war, isn't the human enterprise doomed to failure—even when joined by the most exalted philosophical types? Mustn't Paul be closer to the mark when he says of preborn souls (the same souls Plato is describing in his metaphor of the charioteers): "For whom [God] did foreknow, he also did predestinate to be conformed to the image of his Son, that he might be the firstborn among many brethren. Moreover whom he did predestinate, them he also called: and whom he called, them he also justified: and whom he justified, them he also glorified"? In other words, if we mud-spattered human beings are ever to ascend to Truth, we can do it only because God, a force ineffably greater than our war-torn selves, has predestined us and calls us upward. We will never make it under our own steam.

Having made this connection, Augustine falls apart. What he describes at this point in the *Confessions* is a full-scale emotional breakdown. And all over an idea? Yes, for Augustine ideas do not float free, abstracted from their human context. He personalizes everything, even the most rarefied philosophical utterances. Without education, he would probably have been a self-destructive provincial roustabout, always smoldering with one fire or another. With the discipline of his education, he is transformed into that unusual specimen: neither denatured academic nor effete upper-class connoisseur, but a man of feeling who takes ideas seriously. As with Tolstoy and Joyce, both educated wildmen, the riotous blood of his homeland beats forever in his veins—and animates his every thought.

While talking with his fellow seeker Alypius, he begins to weep uncontrollably. This "mighty shower of tears," as he calls it, comes upon him out of nowhere—"from the secret bottom of my soul." Abashed, he runs from the house into the garden, throwing himself under a fig tree and "giving full vent to my tears." He begins to wail near-nonsense, for no reason he can understand: "And Thou, O Lord, how long? how long, O Lord! Will you stay angry forever?"

From a house bordering the garden, he hears a child's voice, chanting nonsense of its own: *"Tolle, lege, tolle, lege"* ("Take, read, take, read"). Never having heard this children's song before, he decides it is a sign, meant for him. He returns to the house and takes from the table (where the stunned Alypius is still sitting) the book he had been reading earlier, an edition of Paul's letters. In the time-honored fashion of the ancient world, he opens the book at random, intending to receive as a divine message the first sentence his eyes should fall upon. The sentence he reads is: "Not in rioting and drunkenness, not in chambering and wantonness, not in strife and envying; but put ye on the Lord Jesus Christ, and make not provision for the flesh, to fulfill the lusts thereof."

Augustine is caught. He submits himself to the death of the flesh through baptism—and to the Christian God.

We have been using Augustine as a lens for viewing the classical world. What is about to be lost in the century of the barbarian invasions is literature—the content of classical civilization. Had the destruction been complete—had every library been disassembled and every book burned—we might have lost Homer and Virgil and all of classical poetry, Herodotus and Tacitus and all of classical history, Demosthenes and Cicero and all of classical oratory, Plato and Aristotle and all of Greek philosophy, and Plotinus and Porphyry and all the subsequent commentary. We would have lost the taste and smell of a whole civilization. Twelve centuries of lyric beauty, aching tragedy, intellectual inquiry, scholarship, sophistry, and love of Wisdom—the acme of ancient civilized discourse—would all have gone down the drain of history. All but a few lines of Sappho and much of the work of the Greek tragedians—Aeschylus, Sophocles, and Euripides—*did* go down that drain. And we very nearly lost the whole of Latin literature.

We did lose, at any rate, the *spirit* of classical civilization. "At certain epochs," wrote Kenneth Clark in *Civilisation,* "man has felt conscious of something about himself—body and spirit —which was outside the day-to-day struggle for existence and the night-to-night struggle with fear; and he has felt the need to develop these qualities of thought and feeling so that they might approach as nearly as possible to an ideal of perfection— reason, justice, physical beauty, all of them in equilibrium. He has managed to satisfy this need in various ways—through myths, through dance and song, through systems of philosophy and through the order that he has imposed upon the visible world." The struggle for existence and the struggle with fear now gain the ascendancy once more, and what remains of classical civilization will be henceforth found not in life but between the covers of books.

What is really lost when a civilization wearies and grows small is confidence, a confidence built on the order and balance that leisure makes possible. Again, Clark: "Civilisation requires a modicum of material prosperity—enough to provide a little leisure. But, far more, it requires confidence—confidence in the society in which one lives, belief in its philosophy, belief in its laws, and confidence in one's own mental powers. . . . Vigour, energy, vitality: all the great civilisations—or civilising epochs—have had a weight of energy behind them. People sometimes think that civilisation consists in fine sensibilities and good conversation and all that. These can be among the agreeable results of civilisation, but they are not what make a civilisation, and a society can have these amenities and yet be dead and rigid."

Whether insoluble political realities or inner spiritual sickness is more to blame for the fall of classical civilization is, finally, beside the point. The life behind the works we have been studying—the passionate nobility of Virgil, the cool rationality of Cicero, the celestial meditativeness of Plato—this flame of civilization is about to be extinguished. The works themselves will miraculously escape destruction. But they will enter the new world of the Middle Ages as things so strange they might as well have been left behind by interstellar aliens. One example will suffice to illustrate the strangeness of books to medieval men. The word *grammar*—the first step in the course of classical study that molded all educated men from

Plato to Augustine—will be mispronounced by one barbarian tribe as "glamour." In other words, whoever has grammar—whoever can read—possesses magic inexplicable.

So the living civilization died, to be reassembled and assessed by scholars of later ages from the texts preserved miraculously in the pages of its books. There is, however, one classical tradition that survived the transition—the still-living tradition of Roman law.

We have encountered Roman law already—as a dead letter, promulgated by the emperor and circumvented, first by the powerful, then increasingly by anyone who could get away with it. As the emperor's laws become weaker, the ceremony surrounding them becomes more baroque. In the last days, the Divine One's edict is written in gold on purple paper, received with covered hands in the fashion of a priest handling sacred vessels, held aloft for adoration by the assembled throng, who prostrate themselves before the law—and then ignore it.

But this picture alone would be misleading. Just as we found earlier that the ancients had far greater respect than we for practical, public discourse, so they had far greater fear of chaos. The Britons, the Gauls, the Africans, the Slavs who long ago had flocked to the Roman standard, forsaking their petty tribal loyalties and becoming Roman citizens, gained greatly. By exchanging tribal identity for the penumbra of citizenship, they won the protection of the Pax Romana—and its predictability. With the decline of sudden and unexpected violence of all kinds, they could look forward, in a way they had never been able to do before: they could plan, they could prosper, they could expect to live a normal life span.

As Roman culture died out and was replaced by vibrant

new barbarian growths, people forgot many things—how to read, how to think, how to build magnificently—but they remembered and they mourned the lost peace. Call them the people of the Dark Ages if you will, but do not underestimate the desire of these early medieval men and women for the rule of law. There was, moreover, one office that survived intact from the classical to the medieval *polis:* the office of Catholic bishop.

In late antiquity, as municipal and provincial governments disintegrated and imperial appointees abandoned their posts, there was one official who could be counted on to stay with his people, even to death: the *episkopos* (say it quickly and you will hear where the English word *bishop* came from), a Greek word meaning "overseer" or "superintendent." In the Acts of the Apostles and the letters of Paul, bishops are mentioned occasionally as church functionaries, hardly distinguishable from priests (from the Greek *presbyteroi,* or elders). Most early Christian congregations seem to have been run by some combination of bishops and priests, local men—and, in the first stages of development, women as well—who were chosen by the congregants for specified terms to take care of practical matters. With the deaths of the apostles *(apostoloi,* or envoys), who had been the chief conveyors of Jesus's message, the role of the bishop grew; and by the beginning of the second century we find him being treated in a more exalted manner—as a successor to the dead apostles and symbol of unity for the local congregation—but still the appointee of his congregation. As its symbol of unity, he was duty-bound to consult his congregation in all important matters. "From the beginning of my episcopacy," the aristocratic Cyprian of Carthage, monumental bishop of third-century Africa, confided to his clergy, "I made up my mind to do nothing on my own private opinion, without your advice and without the consent of the people."

By the end of Augustine's life, such consultation was becoming the exception. Democracy depends on a well-informed electorate; and bishops could no longer rely on the opinion of their flocks—increasingly, uninformed and harried illiterates—nor, in all likelihood, were they averse to seeing their own power grow at the expense of the people. In many districts, they were already the sole authority left, the last vestige of Roman law and order. They began to appoint one another; and thus was born—five centuries after the death of Jesus—the self-perpetuating hierarchy that rules the Catholic church to this day.

The Roman *polis* had always depended more upon living men than written laws. Laws had to be interpreted and executed; and men of property and standing were allowed much leeway in interpreting the laws. Now, bishops, along with the petty kings and princes of the New World Order, would become the only men of property and standing left. The "king" or local chief was likely to be a barbarian with peculiar notions of justice and few whatever of order. It would become the task of the bishop—often the only man who still had books of any kind and, save for his scribes, the only man who could read and write—to "civilize" the ruler, to introduce to him diplomatically some elementary principles of justice and good government. Thus did the power of the bishop, sometimes himself the only "prince" in sight, continue to wax.

Augustine died as the Vandals besieged the gates of the city he served as bishop, so he didn't live quite long enough to experience the disorderly tempests of this New World Order at their most ripping. Still, his last years were crammed with stress and controversy. Following his conversion, he had hoped to continue in the quiet pursuit of Truth in a philosophical community of like-minded friends. But the stiffness of his backbone, which in a more peaceful age would have retarded his ecclesiastical progress, gave him the appearance of a ready-made bishop—a shepherd of courage, who would not desert his vulnerable flock—and it was only a matter of time before some church drafted him. In the event, it was Hippo, second city of Roman Africa.

If the ancient eastern (or Greek) church has many "fathers" —theologians who articulated the classical formulations of faith to the Greco-Roman world—the ancient western (or Latin) church has only one worth speaking of: Augustine. Out of his interior dialogues with Plato and Paul, he formulated the doctrine of original sin—the sin of Adam and Eve, passed from generation to generation in the fleshly act of generativity. "As in Adam all die, even so in Christ shall all be made alive": Augustine interprets these words of Paul as description of the necessary solidarity of the human race, both in falling hopelessly into sin and rising by grace to redemption. He formulates the doctrine of grace—the gift of God, freely given to men who cannot merit it. He even formulates an explanation of the Trinity. God is One—as in the "Old" Testament, the scripture of the Jews—but at the very heart of reality is relation, the relatedness of friends: for God the One is Three, the Father Who loves the Son, the Son begotten of the Father's love from all eternity, and the holy Spirit—the love of Father and Son, so strong that it forms a third "person" in this divine Trinity.

In 410, Rome, the Eternal City, fell to Alaric the Goth. The moral accusations against the Christian majority by the shrinking pagan community then rose to a final crescendo. Augustine could little appreciate how beside-the-point the pagan criticisms would soon appear. He summons all his powers to write his final masterpiece, *The City of God*, in which human reality is divided in two: Babylon, the City of Man, which necessarily ends in corruption and death, and the New Jerusalem, the City of God, which flourishes eternally beyond all strife. Rome, though better than most human political establishments, is doomed to perish, like all things in the corruptible sphere.

Augustine's enemies are many. He crosses swords with Pelagius, an egregiously fat British monk who posits that God's grace is not always needed, that men, unassisted, can do good with the aid of their rational minds and their goodwill. Pelagius is a sort of Norman Vincent Peale, who thinks everyone who really wants to can pull himself up by his bootstraps. It is a case of Pelagius's "Be all you can be!" versus Augustine's "Just as I am without one plea." Pelagius is also an elitist who believes that some men—the nice, educated ones—are better than others. Augustine smells the Platonic fallacy, the equation of knowledge with virtue, and attacks mercilessly. He scores an easy win.

He is surrounded, as are all the African Catholic bishops of his day, by Donatists, heretics who deny that the grace of the sacraments can be conferred through the offices of an unworthy priest, but in all other respects resemble their Catholic brethren. For Augustine, the sacraments of the church are profoundly necessary: without their aid all men would in their inevitable weakness succumb to evil. Sacramental efficacy simply cannot hinge on the character of the administering priest. Augustine aligns himself with the civil arm to persecute the Donatists and bring them forcibly within the walls of Catholicism. He subsequently writes the first Catholic justification for state persecution of those in error: error has no rights; to disbelieve in forced conversions is to deny the power of God; and God must whip the son he receives—*"per molestias eruditio"* ("true education begins with physical abuse"). This from the man who condemned the "punishments and cruel threats" of his childhood classroom. Augustine, the last great man of Roman antiquity, is going over the edge. The doctrine he has enunciated will echo down the ages in the cruelest infamies, executed with the highest justification. Augustine, father of many firsts, is also father of the Inquisition.

In his old age, Augustine is challenged by Julian of Eclanum, a young, aristocratically educated, married bishop, a species of Pelagian, who finds distasteful Augustine's theories of original sin—or at least some of their implications. Augustine, who, as we saw, believed that God had predestined each of us from all eternity, therefore finds it necessary to assume that God will condemn to hellfire all the unbaptized—even infants who die without the sacrament. Augustine justifies God's justice as inscrutable. Julian counters that Augustine's God is a cruel tyrant. Augustine assumes that original sin is passed along in the very fluids of procreation and that sexual intercourse, because it involves a loss of rational control, is always at least venially sinful—and should be indulged in as little as possible. (Remember how important control—the opposite of chaos— was to the ancients: Augustine's is an argument that could have been made by a Stoic or Buddhist as well as a Christian.) Julian informs Augustine that he has sex with his wife whenever and wherever he feels like it. Augustine explodes:

"Really, really: is that your experience? So you would not

have married couples restrain that evil—I refer of course to your favorite good? So you would have them jump into bed whenever they like, whenever they feel tickled by desire. Far be it from them to postpose this itch till bedtime: let's have your 'legitimate union of bodies' whenever your 'natural good' is excited. If this is the sort of married life you lead, don't drag up your experience in debate!"

Here is Augustine at his Ciceronian worst, arguing without regard to fairness or truth, arguing to win—by the most scurrilous kind of argument, the *ad hominem*. We should not forget that the ancient world, both western and eastern, often found sexual passion—especially in women—an object of mockery and even of contempt. Augustine goes further, and by the end of his life the reformed profligate deems a woman's embraces "sordid, filthy, and horrible." Julian is proposing a new approach, based on his own experience. But he is a rational man, who will not receive his justification till the thought of Thomas Aquinas in the thirteenth century.

Augustine, the feeling man, here shows the limits of feeling when mind has shut down to all that opposes its already established propositions. Augustine lived before the time of crucifixes, confessionals, and statues of the Virgin Mary, but one can imagine that he would have approved of them all. The bloody *corpus* is Augustine himself, splayed like Christ between heaven and earth. The shadows of the confessional would have given him the perfect outlet for his exquisite sympathy toward sinners: against Pelagius's prissy claim that a man is responsible for his every action, Augustine had insisted that "many sins . . . are committed by men weeping and groaning in their distress." Mary, mother of celibate clerics who have turned their back on human love, would have presented Augustine with the perfect heavenly projection of his own domineering mother.

Augustine, for all his greatness, has become in old age the type of the evil cleric, full of mercy for those who fear him, full of seething contempt for those who dare oppose him, scheming to make common cause with Babylon and whatever state-sponsored cruelty will, in the name of Order, suppress his opposition. There is not a country in the world today that does not still possess a few examples of the type.

Meanwhile, on an island off the Atlantic coast that had never heard of Augustine or his battles . . .

III

λ Shifting
World
of
Darkness

Unholy Ireland

There is a plain in northwest Ireland called Rathcroghan,✦ the medieval word *rath* indicating that a notable—and fortified—dwelling once stood there. In the centuries of Ireland's prehistory—before the written word—this place was called Cruachan Ai, and here stood the royal palace from which the province of Connacht was ruled. It was a primitive building, built by local craftsmen from local materials, and yet it was a place that might please our contemporary eye: round, light, two-storied, and held aloft by carved wooden pillars that created a small maze of well-constructed rooms, paneled in red yew, and at its center the royal hall and bedroom—"guarded by screens of copper with bars of silver and gold birds on the screens, and precious jewels in the birds' heads for eyes" (as such a palace was anciently described). Incredibly enough, we have a sort of record of a conversation that once took place in this bedroom. It is as if we can listen in on an exchange that is roughly two millennia old.

The royal bed is laid, and two large figures are reclining there, conversing playfully amid the pillows, as might any man and woman when day is done. Ailil, the king, is musing:

"It is true what they say, love: it is well for the wife of a wealthy man."

"True enough," replies Medb, the queen. "What put that in your mind?"

"It struck me how much better off you are today than the day I married you."

✦ Consult the Pronunciation Guide at the back of the book for pronunciation of certain Irish words.

"I was well enough off without you."

"Then your wealth was something I didn't know or hear much about—except for your woman's things, and the neighboring enemies making off with loot and plunder."

Medb doesn't care for the direction the conversation is taking, and reminding Ailil that her father was high king of Ireland —Eochaid Feidlech the Steadfast—she gives him a quick tour of her genealogy, in case he'd forgotten. Of Eochaid's six daughters, Medb was "highest and haughtiest":

"I outdid them in grace and giving and battle and warlike combat. I had fifteen hundred soldiers in my royal pay, all exiles' sons, and the same number of freeborn native men, and for every paid soldier I had ten more men, and nine more, and eight, and seven, and six, and five, and four, and three, and two, and one. And that was only our ordinary household!"

Clearly stung, she barrels on, letting Ailil know who let whom into this bed:

"My father gave me a whole province of Ireland, *this* province ruled from Cruachan, which is why I am called 'Medb of Cruachan.' " Medb recounts her wooing by the kings of Ireland—"and I wouldn't go. For I asked a harder wedding gift than any woman ever asked before from a man in Ireland—the absence of meanness and jealousy and fear." She had decided Ailil had these qualities and settled on him. "When we were promised, I brought you the best wedding gift a bride can bring: apparel enough for a dozen men, a chariot worth thrice seven bondmaids, the width of your face of red gold and the weight of your left arm of light gold. So, if anyone causes you shame or upset or trouble, the right to compensation is mine, for you're a kept man."

Ailil responds hotly that he has two kings for brothers and

that he "*let* them rule because they were older, not because they are better than I am in grace and giving. I never heard, in all Ireland, of a province run by a woman except this one, which is why I came and took the kingship here."

"It still remains," says Medb between her teeth, "that my fortune is greater than yours."

"You amaze me. No one has more," shouts Ailil, gesturing grandly, "than I have, and I know it!"

All right, then, they must take inventory! That very night:

the lowliest of their possessions were brought out to see who had more property and jewels and precious things: their buckets and tubs and iron pots, jugs and wash-pails and vessels with handles. Then their finger-rings, brace-lets, thumb-rings, and gold treasures were brought out, and their cloths of purple, blue, black, green and yellow, plain grey and many-colored, yellow-brown, checked and striped. Their herds of sheep were taken in off the fields and meadows and plains. They were measured and matched, and found to be the same in numbers and size. Even the great ram leading Medb's sheep, the worth of one bondmaid by himself, had a ram to match him lead-ing Ailil's sheep.

From pasture and paddock their teams and herds of horses were brought in. For the finest stallion in Medb's stud, worth one bondmaid by himself, Ailil had a stallion to match. Their vast herds of pigs were taken in from the woods and gullies and waste places. They were measured and matched and noted, and Medb had one fine boar, but Ailil had another. Then their droves and free-wandering herds of cattle were brought in from the woods and wastes of the province. These were matched and measured and noted also, and found to be the same in number and size. But there was one great bull in Ailil's herd, that had been a calf of one of Medb's cows—Finnbennach was his name, the White Horned—and Finnbennach, refusing to be led by a woman, had gone over to the king's herd. Medb couldn't find in her herd the equal of this bull, and her spirits dropped as though she hadn't a single penny.

How do we come by this extraordinary encounter? Can we depend, at all, on its accuracy?

I have been quoting from the first scene of the Irish prose epic *Tain Bo Cuailnge, The Cattle Raid of Cooley.* There are several versions, none of them complete, the earliest dating to the eighth century. This scene comes to us from a twelfth-century manuscript, translated masterfully from the ancient Irish by the contemporary Irish poet Thomas Kinsella. The manuscript tradition, however, is based on an earlier oral tradition that may go back to the time of Christ. And though we can hardly claim to have this royal conversation word for word, the oral-scribal tradition witnesses that such a conversation may well have been the impetus for the rest of the epic action of the *Tain.*

Medb calls for the chief messenger, Mac Roth, and asks where the match of Ailil's bull might be found. "I know where to find such a bull and better," Mac Roth tells her, "in the province of Ulster, in the territory of Cuailnge, in Daire mac Fiachna's house. Donn Cuailnge is the bull's name, the Brown Bull of Cuailnge."

"Go there, Mac Roth," orders Medb. "Ask Daire to lend

me Donn Cuailnge for a year. At the end of the year he can have fifty yearling heifers in payment for the loan, and the Brown Bull of Cuailnge back. And you can offer him this too, Mac Roth, if the people of the country think badly of losing their fine jewel, the Donn Cuailnge: if Daire himself comes with the bull I'll give him a portion of the fine Plain of Ai equal to his own lands, and a chariot worth thrice seven bondmaids, and my own friendly thighs on top of that."

The reader is not surprised when Daire graciously accepts this deal! Unfortunately, Daire's generous hospitality to Mac Roth's party undoes the agreement, for "they were given the best of good food and kept supplied with the festive fare until they grew drunk and noisy." The messengers then get into a verbal duel about whether Medb's forces could have taken the Brown Bull from Ulster by force, had Daire not agreed to the transaction. Daire's steward enters the room just as one boasts: "We would have taken it anyway, with or without his leave!"

With that, the deal is off. "And only it isn't my habit," smolders Daire after he has learned of the drunken boast, "to murder messengers or travelers or any other wayfarers, not one of you would leave here alive."

When Mac Roth recounts this outcome to Medb, she announces genially: "We needn't polish the knobs and knots in this, Mac Roth. It was well known it would be taken by force if it wasn't given freely. And taken it will be." Medb assembles a vast army, which under her command sets out forthwith for Cuailnge to capture the Brown Bull. En route they will be met not by the forces of Ulster, who have been laid low by mysterious pangs, but by one champion only, the boy Cuchulainn.

The first thing that will probably strike any modern reader

who opens the *Tain* is what a rough, strange world this is, both simple and full of barbaric splendor. Here is no deliberation or subtlety, no refinement or ambiguity. We know immediately that we are at a far remove from Virgil, Cicero, Plato, and the whole literary tradition of the classical world, excepting perhaps Homer. The characters of the *Tain* do not think profoundly; they do not seem to think at all. But they do act—and with a characteristic panache and roundedness that easily convinces us of their humanity.

And none more rounded than Medb. How different a queen she is from Dido. One cannot see Medb languishing for a lover—or for anything. If Augustine was the first self-conscious man, Medb—at the other end of the consciousness spectrum—is prereflective. Her ready speech, moreover, is characteristically Irish. We can imagine her sharp first sentence ("What put that in your mind?") on the lips of many a character in modern Irish drama—and this opens up to us an astonishing continuity: from prehistoric Ireland to the present day.

The sexual frankness of these characters is unlike anything in classical literature, even in the folk epics of Homer. We would need to reach all the way back to the Sumerian *Epic of Gilgamesh* to find anything comparable. Medb's offer of "her two friendly thighs" to seal the bargain with Daire is obviously thrown in casually. And it is just as obvious that Medb is not in the remotest sense a needy woman—the very phrase would curdle before her! Rather, in early Irish literature both men and women openly admire one another's physical endowments and invite one another to bed without formality.

In another story, Derdriu—Deirdre of the Sorrows—passes Noisiu on the rampart of Emain Macha, the chief seat of the

Ulster kings. They have never seen each other before. Of Derdriu, the king's druid, Cathbad, had prophesied that

> High queens will ache with envy
> to see those lips of Parthian-red
> opening on her pearly teeth,
> and see her pure perfect body.

Though Noisiu knows that she is pledged to the old king and that there is a curse on her, he cannot help himself: "That is a fine heifer going by."

"As well it might," Derdriu shoots back. "The heifers grow big where there are no bulls."

"You have the bull of this province all to yourself—the king of Ulster."

"Of the two, I'd pick a game young bull like you."

Guess what happens next.

Similarly, there is recorded in another story of the *Tain* cycle this conversation between the boy Cuchulainn, the Irish Achilles, and Emer, the girl he comes to woo:

"May your road be blessed!" cries Emer on his approach.

"May the apple of your eye see only good," returns Cuchulainn. Then, peering down her dress: "I see a sweet country. I could rest my weapon there."

The tasks the hero must perform before this sweet country is open to him are laid out by Emer herself—not by her father, as would be the case in a continental fairy tale:

"No man will travel this country until he has killed a hundred men at every ford from Scenmenn ford on the river Ailbine, to Banchuing . . . where the frothy Brea makes Fedelm leap."

"In that sweet country I'll rest my weapon."

"No man will travel this country until he has done the feat of the salmon-leap carrying twice his weight in gold, and struck down three groups of nine men with a single stroke, leaving the middle man of each nine unharmed."

"In that sweet country I'll rest my weapon."

"No man will travel this country who hasn't gone sleepless from Samain [Hallowe'en], when summer goes to its rest, until Imbolc [Candlemas or Groundhog Day], when the ewes are milked at spring's beginning; from Imbolc to Beltaine [May Day] at the summer's beginning and from Beltaine to Bron Trogain, earth's sorrowing autumn."

"It is said and done."

Well, they may not be civilized, but they certainly are confident—and this confidence is one of the open-handed pleasures of early Irish literature. We have no trouble imagining these people, both men and women, riding hard on horseback, drawing the blood of their enemies, leaping about in muscular dancing, and passing the damp Irish night in vigorous coupling. Even their sorrows and deaths are tossed off with a shrug, though they understand tragedy and receive it as convulsively as any people. "For the great Gaels of Ireland," wrote G. K. Chesterton,

Are the men that God made mad.
For all their wars are merry,
And all their songs are sad.

The Irish are part of a larger ethnic grouping called the Celts (preferably pronounced with a hard "c"), who first entered western consciousness about 600 B.C.—only a century and a half after the legendary founding of the City of Rome— when, like the German barbarians long after them, they crossed the Rhine. One branch of the Celtic tree settled in present-day France and became the Gauls, whom Julius Caesar would conquer in the century before Christ and who in their Romanized phase would produce the effete Ausonius. A cognate tribe settled the Iberian peninsula and became great sea traders; indeed, traces of the buildings of these Iberian Celts may have been found as far afield as New Hampshire—which would make the Celts the first Europeans to reach the Americas. In the third century B.C., Celts invaded the Greek world, advancing as far south as Delphi and settling in present-day Turkey, where, as the Galatians (note the similarity of consonantal sounds in "Celt," "Gaul," and "Galatian"), they were recipients of one of Paul's letters. Siblings of the Gaulish Celts crossed to Britain as early as 400 B.C., becoming the Britons, who nine centuries later, in the time of Augustine and Patricius, would be gradually pushed by the Angles and Saxons into Cornwall, where they would become the Cornish, and into Wales, where they would become the Welsh. It is from these British Celts that the legends of King Arthur and the Knights of the Round Table would spring. Echoes of the language they spoke may be heard today in the form of modern Welsh and Breton, which belong to the same linguistic group as Gaulish.

About 350 B.C., some fifty years after Celtic tribes began their invasion of Britain, they reached Ireland. Some, no doubt, came by way of Britain, but it is most likely that those who gained ascendancy were Iberian Celts, whose language was somewhat different from that of the British invaders. These became in time the Irish; and the language they spoke belongs not to the Brythonic branch of Welsh and Breton but to a Celtic branch called Goidelic by scholars—whose present-day shoots are the last living Gaelic tongues: Irish and Scots Gaelic. Ireland itself is the only Celtic nation-state in our world, all the other Celts having been absorbed by larger political entities.

In the Irish foundation myth, the sons of Mil, survivors of the Great Flood through their descent from Noah, reach Ireland from Spain and wrest it from a tribe called Tuatha De Danaan, the People of the Goddess Danu. The connection to Noah can only be the result of later monkish tinkering with the original material—somehow, the Irish had to be connected to things biblical. But there is little reason to doubt the Iberian connection. We have evidence that the Tuatha De Danaan have some historical reality, as well: we know that Ireland was peopled before the arrival of the Celts in the fourth century B.C. and that an earlier people had built the great barrows and magnificently carved tumuli that dot the Irish landscape to this day. In the foundation myth, the Tuatha De Danaan are preternaturally skilled in building and craftsmanship. These taller, otherworldly beings eventually devolve into "the little people," the fairies and leprechauns of later Irish legend, whose spirits haunt the tombs and fairy mounds they once built. "The little people" is a euphemism—rather like the prehistoric phrase *le bon dieu*—meant to disguise the speaker's fear of something unfamiliar and much larger than himself. It is possible that this flickering phenomenon of the little people represents the afterglow of Irish guilt over their exploitation of more artful aborigines.

Even at this early stage of their development, the Irish were intoxicated by the power of words. Every noble Irish family maintained a family of ancestral poets. The sons of Mil were accompanied by their poet, Amhairghin, who, stepping off the boat that brought him to the Irish shore, proclaimed:

I am an estuary into the sea.
I am a wave of the ocean.
I am the sound of the sea.
I am a powerful ox.
I am a hawk on a cliff.
I am a dewdrop in the sun.
I am a plant of beauty.
I am a boar for valour.
I am a salmon in a pool.
I am a lake in a plain.
I am the strength of art.

One problem with this Irish prehistoric material is that we cannot date it with any precision. From the Celtic invasion in the fourth century B.C. to the invasion of books nine centuries later, after which the traditional oral lore began to be written down, we are looking at a timeless Ireland. We can presume that Amhairghin's poem, at least in its current form, is not actually as old as the Celtic invasion, but we cannot be sure how old it is. We can date the action of the *Táin* perhaps to the first century of our era, perhaps to a century or so later, but there is no way of knowing when this episode or that was added to the strand of narrative.

What hints we have suggest that Ireland was, during this entire period, a land outside of time—that, in fact, it changed little from the time of Amhairghin to the time of Augustine. This was an illiterate, aristocratic, seminomadic, Iron Age warrior culture, its wealth based on animal husbandry and slavery (the importance of both of which one cannot fail to notice in the *Tain*'s royal inventory). Such cultures have been known to exist for many hundreds of years without undergoing appreciable alteration. What normally changes them is outside influence, rather than inner dynamics; and Ireland, splendidly isolated in the Atlantic and largely beyond the traffic of civilization, suffered few intrusive influences. We can safely assume, therefore, that the world of Medb and Ailil was little different from the earlier Ireland that the Celtic invaders had made and that this world, in most respects, remained intact into the century of Rome's fall. On this timeless island, one would have come in contact with a culture very like that of the British and continental Celts prior to their centuries of Roman influence. In this place and period, one might also have experienced a milieu *something* like such pre-Roman cultures as Homeric Greece, the India of the *Mahabharata,* and Sumer, with their common equipage of warhorses and warrior chariots and their common standards of heroic action.

The Irish, like all the Celts, stripped before battle and rushed their enemy naked, carrying sword and shield but wearing only sandals and torc—a twisted, golden neck ornament. Just such a torc may be seen around the neck of the naked *Dying Gaul,* a Greek statue of the third century B.C. The Gaul's tough hide has been pierced by a heart wound between his ribs, and he is bleeding to death. Sitting on the ground, he holds himself erect with a last effort of will. His face is a drama of both dignity and hopelessness, as he "casts a cold eye on life, on death." The Romans, in their first encounters with these exposed, insane warriors, were shocked and frightened. Not only were the men naked, they were howling and, it seemed, possessed by demons, so outrageous were their strength and verve.

Urged on by the infernal skirl of pipers, they presented to the unaccustomed and throbbing Roman sensorium a multimedia event featuring all the terrors of hell itself.

The Irish heroes were aware that they became possessed when confronted by the enemy and that their appearances could alter considerably, and they called this phenomenon the "warp-spasm." When in the *Tain* the armies of Connacht are confronted by Ulster's champion, the seventeen-year-old Cuchulainn, this is how he appears:

The first warp-spasm seized Cuchulainn, and made him into a monstrous thing, hideous and shapeless, un-heard of. His shanks and his joints, every knuckle and angle and organ from head to foot, shook like a tree in the flood or a reed in the stream. His body made a furious twist inside his skin, so that his feet and shins and knees switched to the rear and his heels and calves switched to the front. The balled sinews of his calves switched to the front of his shins, each big knot the size of a warrior's bunched fist. On his head the temple-sinews stretched to the nape of his neck, each mighty, immense, measureless knob as big as the head of a month-old child. His face and features became a red bowl: he sucked one eye so deep into his head that a wild crane couldn't probe it onto his cheek out of the depths of his skull; the other eye fell out along his cheek. His mouth weirdly distorted: his cheek peeled back from his jaws until the gullet appeared, his lungs and liver flapped in his mouth and throat, his lower jaw struck the upper a lion-killing blow, and fiery flakes large as a ram's fleece reached his mouth from his throat. His heart boomed loud in his breast like the baying of a watch-dog at its feed or the sound of a lion among bears. Malignant mists and spurts of fire—the torches of Badb— flickered red in the vaporous clouds that rose boiling above his head, so fierce was his fury. The hair of his head twisted like the tangle of a red thornbush stuck in a gap; if a royal apple tree with all its kingly fruit were shaken above him, scarce an apple would reach the ground but each would be spiked on a bristle of his hair as it stood up on his scalp with rage. The hero-halo rose out of his brow, long and broad as a warrior's whetstone, long as a snout, and he went mad rattling his shields, urging on his charioteer and harassing the hosts. Then, tall and thick, steady and strong, high as the mast of a noble ship, rose up from the dead centre of his skull a straight spout of black blood darkly and magically smoking like the smoke from a royal hostel when a king is coming to be cared for at the close of a winter day.

In a word, a formidable opponent. Blithe exaggeration is a regular feature of Irish heroic literature, a convention as enjoyable to its intended audience as the exaggerations of a sportscaster to a Super Bowl audience. As in so many passages from the *Táin,* this one yields up a vivid miniature of the period—in the near-Homeric simile describing a warm and welcoming hostel on a winter's evening. More than this, we glimpse something of the emotional temper of these people and the high pitch of feeling at which their lives were lived. I do not question for a second that the warp-spasm was a real experience, keenly felt by its subject and plainly observable to the opposing army. Anyone who has ever felt (or been the object of) real rage can understand the distortions described in this passage.

As, I think, can anyone who has experienced terror: what a perfect ritual for dealing with the warrior's own terror, as the booming of the heart within his breast is transformed into "the baying of a watch-dog at its feed" and he himself is transformed from ordinary mortal into killing machine:

> [Cuchulainn then] went into the middle of them and beyond, and mowed down great ramparts of his enemies' corpses, circling completely around the armies three times, attacking them in hatred. They fell sole to sole and neck to headless neck, so dense was that destruction. He circled them three times more in the same way, and left a bed of them six deep in a great circuit, the soles of three to the necks of three in a circle round the camp. . . . Any count or estimate of the rabble who fell there is unknown, and unknowable. Only the names of the chiefs have been counted. . . . In this great Carnage on Murtheimne Plain Cuchulainn slew one hundred and thirty kings, as well as an uncountable horde of dogs and horses, women and boys and children and rabble of all kinds. Not one man in three escaped without his thighbone or his head or his eye being smashed, or without some blemish for the rest of his life. And when the battle was over Cuchulainn left without a scratch or a stain on himself, his helper or either of his horses.

More often than not, Cuchulainn reminds us of a comic book hero. The only audience likely to be amazed by exploits like these today would be preadolescent boys—but then in early stories like the *Tain,* we touch the imaginative childhood of the human race. Even the hero's gear suggests such a connection. Here, for instance, is the description of Cuchulainn's chariot:

When the spasm had run through the high hero Cuchulainn he stepped into his sickle war-chariot that bristled with points of iron and narrow blades, with hooks and hard prongs, and heroic frontal spikes, with ripping instruments and tearing nails on its shafts and straps and loops and cords. The body of the chariot was spare and slight and erect, fitted for the feats of a champion, with space for the lordly warrior's eight weapons, speedy as the wind or as a swallow or a deer darting over the level plain. The chariot was settled down on two fast steeds, wild and wicked, neat-headed and narrow bodied, with slender quarters and roan breast, firm in hoof and harness—a notable sight in the trim chariot-shafts. One horse was lithe and swift-leaping, high-arched and powerful, long-bodied and with great hooves. The other flowing-maned and shining, slight and slender in hoof and heel. In that style, then, he drove out to find his enemies.

How these people would have loved the Batmobile! But while they are hypnotized by physical display, calculation is beyond them. The numbers of the dead—as of the living—are considerably inflated: nothing like a real accounting is attempted. These counts are not dissimilar to the ages of the centuries-old patriarchs found in the Book of Genesis. All the storyteller really wants to say is that the number of dead was astonishingly large—or that Methuselah lived a very long time.

Throughout the early centuries of our era, human settlements were far smaller than they are today. The population of a great city or a small country could be counted in the thousands, and between the settled places lay unpeopled wildernesses, owned by no one in particular, which offered perils to conventional travelers but sanctuaries for the dispossessed. When Medb and Ailil call for their pigs and cattle, these are brought in from the "woods and wastes"—the no-man's-lands, the places in between.

No character in the *Tain* is drawn as perceptively as Medb. She is so full of life and color that even Cuchulainn seems pale beside her. When Fingin the Healer comes to the sorely wounded Cethern, he points to Cethern's largest wound: "A vain, arrogant woman gave you that wound."

"I believe you are right," replies Cethern. "A tall, fair, long-faced woman with soft features came at me. She had a head of yellow hair, and two gold birds on her shoulders. She wore a purple cloak folded about her, with five hands' breadth of gold on her back. She carried a light, stinging, sharp-edged lance in her hand, and she held an iron sword with a woman's grip over her head—a massive figure."

The "massive figure" of Medb dominates the *Tain* as does no other woman in any epic we have left to us. In the *Iliad* Helen makes her cameo appearance; in the *Aeneid* Dido has an interesting supporting role. But the only women in classical literature who impel the story forward are to be found in Greek drama: Clytemnestra, Antigone, Medea. (There are ways in which the *Tain* seems closer to drama than to Homeric epic: it is full of dialogue and short on poetry—which appears only occasionally and, for the most part, in archaic incantations not unlike the choruses of Greek plays.)

The Greek drama of the fifth century B.C. grew out of the seasonal liturgies of an agricultural people and magnified the conflicts of their social life—thus the necessity of significant female characters. But one cannot imagine a woman in Greece's heroic age—that is, three or four centuries before the dramatists, in the period of Greece's early development most comparable to that of the *Tain*—standing on the Trojan battlefield or traveling with Odysseus. Just as unthinkable would be a woman traveling with Aeneas. At the end of the *Tain,* its ostensible moral is uttered by the vaguely omniscient Fergus: "We followed the rump of a misguiding woman. It is the usual thing for a herd led by a mare to be strayed and destroyed." Medb does not reappear after this judgment on her, but even this "last word" seems ontologically overshadowed by her personality.

Nor is she an exception in this literature. Cuchulainn is trained in battlecraft by three women, each more extraordinary than the one before. The god of war, mentioned briefly in the *Tain,* is put in the shade by the three goddesses of war, who regularly make the scene and stir things up. (One of these, Badb, is mentioned in the description of Cuchulainn's warp-spasm.) Derdriu, pledged to Conchobor, the Ulster king, runs off with Noisiu and his brothers—the sons of Uisliu—only to be tracked down and recaptured, as Noisiu is slain. Though she submits to Conchobor, Derdriu never smiles again. Conchobor, out of spite, decides to share her with Eogan mac Durthacht, the king of Fernmag, who to win favor with Conchobor had killed Noisiu—not in a fair fight but through trickery. "They set out the next day for the fair of Macha. She was behind Eogan in the chariot. She had sworn that two men alive in the world together would never have her.

" 'This is good, Derdriu,' Conchobor said. 'Between me and Eogan you are a sheep eyeing two rams.'

"A big block of stone was in front of her. She let her head

be driven against the stone, and made a mass of fragments of it, and she was dead."

A suicide, all right, but nothing like Dido's. These are all women who, in life and death, exhibit the power of their will and the strength of their passion. Here is part of Derdriu's lament for Noisiu, spoken to the royal musicians who had come to cheer her up:

Sweet in your sight the fiery stride
of raiding men returned to Emain.
More nobly strode the three proud
sons of Uisliu toward their home:

Noisiu bearing the best mead
—I would wash him by the fire—
Ardan, with a stag or a boar,
Anle, shouldering his load.

The son of Nes [i.e., King Conchobor], battle-proud,
drinks, you say, the choicest mead.
Choicer still—a brimming sea—
I have taken frequently.

Modest Noisiu would prepare
a cooking-pit in the forest floor.
Sweeter then than any meat
the son of Uisliu's, honey sweet.

Though for you the times are sweet
with pipers and with trumpeters,

I swear today I can't forget
that I have known far sweeter airs.

. . .

Noisiu: his grave-mound is made
and mournfully accompanied.
The highest hero—and I poured
the deadly drink when he died.

His cropped gold fleece I loved,
and fine form—a tall tree.
Alas, I needn't watch today,
nor wait for the son of Uisliu.

I loved the modest, mighty warrior,
loved his fitting, firm desire,
loved him at daybreak as he dressed
by the margin of the forest.

Those blue eyes that melted women,
and menaced enemies, I loved:
then, with our forest journey done,
his chanting through the dark woods.

I don't sleep now,
nor redden my fingernails.
What have I to do with welcomes?
The son of Indel will not come.

The tenacious persistence of certain patterns and emotions in the Irish literary tradition skirts the incredible. Here is part of another lament, composed by another woman for her murdered husband—*eighteen* centuries after Derdriu!

My love and my delight,
The day I saw you first
Beside the markethouse
I had eyes for nothing else
And love for none but you.

.   .   .

You gave me everything.
There were parlours whitened for me
Bedrooms painted for me
Ovens reddened for me,
Loaves baked for me,
Joints spitted for me,
Beds made for me
To take my ease on flock
Until the milking time
And later if I pleased.

.   .   .

My love and my fortune
'Tis an evil portion
To lay for a giant—
A shroud and a coffin—
For a big-hearted hero

Who fished in the hill-streams
And drank in bright halls
With white-breasted women.

.   .   .

My rider of the bright eyes,
What happened you yesterday?
I thought you in my heart,
When I bought you your fine clothes,
A man the world could not slay.

What happened to the rider of the bright eyes is that he
was shot dead by a grasping Englishman one night in 1773,
because he had refused to sell his splendid mare for the paltry
offer of five pounds. By this time, English occupiers had en-
acted the anti-Catholic Penal Laws; among many injustices,
these forbade a Catholic Irishman from owning a horse worth
more than that sum. The slain man was Art O'Leary, an officer
in the army of Maria Theresa of Austria and scion of one of
the last noble Catholic families to survive in Ireland. (As a
Catholic, he could not receive an Irish military commission.)
The poet, his wife, was Dark Eileen O'Connell, an aunt of
Daniel O'Connell, who fifty-seven years later would force
Catholic Emancipation on the English Parliament, becoming a
kind of Irish Catholic Martin Luther King. Her lament is almost the last great poem to be written in the Irish language,
just as the Gaelic order and the old nobility that traced itself
back to the time of Medb and Ailil sank beneath the waves of
English oppression.

Are not the two laments remarkably similar in both imagery and feeling? Derdriu belongs to a simpler time: her excited admiration for the body of her lover, who roasts game for her in their forest shelter, is frank and pure. Dark Eileen is more refined: her husband prepares an entire household for her (with some of the delicacy of an English nursery rhyme), and the sexual feeling is less direct. Both cast a watchful eye on other females! But the strength of Eileen's connection to prehistoric Derdriu becomes especially evident as one searches in vain through eighteenth-century English literature *by women* to find anything so frank and passionate as "The Lament for Art O'Leary." Eileen does not destroy herself directly as did her ancient counterpart, but she comes from the same hard, unbending stock:

'Tis known to Jesus Christ
Nor cap upon my head,
Nor shift upon my back,
Nor shoe upon my foot,
Nor gear in all my house,
Nor bridle for the mare
But I will spend at law;
And I'll go oversea
To plead before the King,
And if the King be deaf⊷
I'll settle things alone
With the black-blooded rogue
That killed my man on me.

Art O'Leary lies buried in the ruined nave of Kilcrea Abbey in

⊷ Which will surely be the case, the king being George III.

County Cork. These words, carved in modern English on his tomb, bring us back to prehistoric Ireland:

LO ARTHUR LEARY

GENROUS HANDSOME BRAVE

SLAIN IN HIS BLOOM

LIES IN THIS HUMBLE GRAVE

The three adjectives—"genrous, handsome, brave"—used to describe the murdered man are a summation of the Iron Age moral code, a code that shines out clearly in all early literature (whether *Gilgamesh,* the *Iliad,* or the *Tain)* and that mysteriously survived in Ireland long after its oblivion in more sophisticated civilizations—and that endures to some extent even to this day.

Recall Medb's boastful self-description: "I outdid [all my sisters] in grace and giving and battle and warlike combat." "Grace": therefore, she is *handsome* (or beautiful). "Giving": therefore, she is *generous.* "Battle and warlike combat": therefore, she is *brave.* Consider the high standards she set for her husband: "the absence of meanness and jealousy and fear." "Meanness" is the opposite of *generosity;* "fear" is the opposite of *bravery.* "Jealousy," though not precisely the logical opposite of *handsomeness,* is eternally linked to it in hopeless conflict: a wife's beauty inevitably provokes the insecure husband to mindless jealousy—not of his wife but of his possible rivals.

But there is also an unnamed virtue, hidden in these trinities: loyalty or faithfulness. Dark Eileen would have been unlikely to carve "genrous, faithful, brave": O'Leary, a handsome figure in his mid-twenties, was known to enjoy, as Eileen herself wrote, drinking "in bright halls with white-breasted women." Nor is faithfulness a virtue Medb could credibly have lauded (though its subterranean existence is hinted at in the jealousy motif). In the heroic eras of various societies, including Ireland's, loyalty served as the foundation virtue. But it is not the insignia of heterosexual unions; rather, it is the bedrock of same-sex friendships. In *Gilgamesh,* there is the unbreakable friendship between Gilgamesh and Enkidu. In the *Iliad,* there is the undying bond between Achilles and Patroclus. In the *Táin,* the only relationship that is presented as ideal is the one between the warriors Cuchulainn and Ferdia, foster brothers who, though forced by Medb's trickery to fight each other, love each other to the end. Thus, Cuchulainn to Ferdia:

> Fast friends, forest-companions,
> we made one bed and slept one sleep
> in foreign lands after the fray.
> Scathach's pupils, two together
> we'd set forth to comb the forest.

> .   .   .

> There is no man that ever ate,
> no man that was ever born,
> no joyous son of king or queen,
> for whose sake I would do you harm.

After he has killed Ferdia, Cuchulainn addresses the corpse:

> When we were away with Scathach
> learning victory overseas,
> it seemed our friendship would remain
> unbroken till the day of doom.

I loved the noble way you blushed,
and loved your fine, perfect form.
I loved your blue clear eye,
your way of speech, your skillfulness[,]

.   .   .

your curled yellow hair
like a great lovely jewel,
the soft leaf-shaped belt
that you wore at your waist.

You have fallen to the Hound,*
I cry for it, little calf.
The shield didn't save you
that brought you to the fray.

The lyrical similarities among the laments of Derdriu, Cuchulainn, and Dark Eileen can hardly be lost on the reader. But only in Cuchulainn's dirge is the value of never-ending faithfulness sung—"fast friends," whose "friendship would remain unbroken till the day of doom." The irony of the speaker, who swore to his foster brother that "there is no man . . . for whose sake I would do you harm," is painful.

Fixity escaped these people, as in the end it escapes us all. They understood, as few have understood before or since, how fleeting life is and how pointless to try to hold on to things or people. They pursued the wondrous deed, the heroic gesture: fighting, fucking, drinking, art —poetry for intense emotion, the

---

* The name Cuchulainn means Culann's Hound.

music that accompanied the heroic drinking with which each day ended, bewitching ornament for one's person and possessions. All these are worth pursuit, and the first, especially, will bring the honor great souls seek. But in the midst of this furious swirl of energy lies a still point of detachment. When, in the heat of battle, the bloodied messenger informs Medb timidly that Cuchulainn has beheaded her son, she responds, "This isn't like catching birds," as we might say, "You didn't think this would be a picnic, did you?" The face of the *Dying Gaul* speaks for them all: each one of us will die, naked and alone, on some battlefield not of our own choosing. My promise of undying faithfulness to you and yours to me, though made with all solemnity, is unlikely to survive the tricks that fate has in store—all the hidden land mines that beset human life. What we can rely on are the comeliness and iron virtue of the short-lived hero: his loyalty to cause and comrades, his bravery in the face of overwhelming odds, the gargantuan generosity with which he scatters his possessions and his person and with which he spills his blood. After the assassination of John F. Kennedy, Daniel Patrick Moynihan was heard to say that to be Irish is to know that in the end the world will break your heart.

Such an outlook and such a temperament make for wonderful songs and thrilling stories, but not for personal peace or social harmony. Though Medb and Ailil, Derdriu and Noisiu would have been exciting to know, they could not have been fun to work for. To such a view—the view of the servant—we now turn: to Patricius, the kidnapped boy shepherding sheep on a bleak Antrim hillside.

I V

Good News
from
Far Off

The First Missionary

No man is a hero to his valet. Still less could an Iron Age Irish warrior be a hero to his British slave, a boy who had spent his first sixteen years amid the comfort and predictability of a Roman *civitas*.

If Cuchulainn slew "one hundred and thirty kings" on Murtheimne Plain, Ireland must have had hundreds of such kings—to one of whom Patricius was bound. His name was Miliucc, and of him we know nothing but that he ruled some hills of Antrim between Lough Neagh and the mountains of Sliabh Mis. *Ri,* the Irish word for king, is cognate with the Latin *rex,* but—to our eyes, at least—these kings would appear to be petty chieftains, local strongmen ruling over a few dozen extended families of cattle ranchers. "Rustlers" might be more accurate, for here was little right except might. The epic depredations of the *Tain* are, after all, but enlargements of a common way: cattle raids, directed by one noble family against another, were among the events of daily life.

The life of a shepherd-slave could not have been a happy one. Ripped out of civilization, Patricius had for his only protector a man who did not hold his own life highly, let alone anyone else's. The work of such shepherds was bitterly isolated, months at a time spent alone in the hills. The occasional contacts, which one might normally seek out, could bring their own difficulties. Deprived of intercourse with other humans, Patricius must have taken a long time to master the language and customs of his exile, so that the approach of strangers over the hills may have held special terror.

We know that he did have two constant companions, hunger and nakedness, and that the gnawing in his belly and the chill on his exposed skin were his worst sufferings, acutely painful presences that could not be shaken off. From this scant information—Patricius is not a man of many words—we can deduce that the boy had a hardy constitution and had probably been a beloved and well-nourished child; otherwise, he could not have survived.

Like many another in impossible circumstances, he began to pray. He had never before paid attention to the teachings of his religion; he tells us that he didn't really believe in God, and he found priests foolish. But now, there was no one to turn to but the God of his parents. One is reminded of the reports of contemporary hostages about how they make it through the dreary years of captivity. "Tending flocks was my daily work, and I would pray constantly during the daylight hours. The love of God and the fear of him surrounded me more and more —and faith grew and the Spirit was roused, so that in one day I would say as many as a hundred prayers and after dark nearly as many again, even while I remained in the woods or on the mountain. I would wake and pray before daybreak—through snow, frost, rain—nor was there any sluggishness in me (such as I experience nowadays) because then the Spirit within me was ardent."

Patricius endured six years of this woeful isolation, and by the end of it he had grown from a careless boy to something he would surely never otherwise have become—a holy man, indeed a visionary for whom there was no longer any rigid separation between this world and the next. On his last night as Miliucc's slave, he received in sleep his first otherworldly experience. A mysterious voice said to him: "Your hungers are rewarded: you are going home."

Patricius sat up, startled. The voice continued: "Look, your ship is ready."

Miliucc's farm was inland, nowhere near the sea, but Patricius set out, whither he knew not. He walked some two hundred miles, through territory he had never covered before, without being stopped or followed, and reached a southeastern inlet, probably near Wexford, where he saw his ship. As he tramped toward his destiny, his faith that he was under God's protection must have grown and grown, for it was virtually impossible that a fugitive slave could get so far without being intercepted. "I came in God's strength . . . and had nothing to fear" is Patricius's simple summation.

The sailors were loading a cargo of Irish hounds for sale on the continent, where they were highly prized. Patricius approached the captain, who eyed him suspiciously. He showed the captain that he had the wherewithal for his passage (where he got it we'll never know!), but the captain told him curtly: "You're wasting your time asking to sail with us."

This was Patricius's moment of greatest danger: recognized as a fugitive in a seaside settlement, he could not expect to remain at liberty many minutes more. "Hearing this response, I left them to go to the hut where I was staying, and on the way I began to pray and before I had finished my prayer I heard one of the sailors shouting after me: 'Come quickly, they're calling you!' And right away I returned to them and they began to say to me: 'Come on board, we'll take you on trust.'" They even offered their nipples to be sucked, the ancient Irish version of "kiss and make up." Patricius, too much the Roman for such *outré* goings-on, held back—he says "for fear of God," but better minds than Patricius's have succumbed to a confusion of Roman custom and Christian faith. The sailors shrugged: "You can make friends with us however you like." Patricius jumped on board, and they sailed at once.

It took three days to cross to the continent, and as they left their ship and journeyed inland they found only devastation— *"desertum,"* Patricius calls it—through which they trudged for two weeks. Where on the continent is there a desert that takes hardy sailors two weeks to cross? Nowhere. But this may well have been the year 407—the very year that hundreds of thousands of hungry Germans had crossed the icy Rhine, wreaking devastation through much of Gaul. Irish sailors would have been unlikely to have heard news of this invasion, so the little party of exporters may have arrived in the wake of the German war parties. At any rate, they can discover neither a single human being nor a meal. The dogs, as well as the men, are close to expiring, "collapsed and half-dead by the side of the road."

"How about it, Christian?" taunts the captain. "You say your god is great and all-powerful, so why can't you pray for us? We're starving to death, and there's little chance of our ever seeing a living soul!" It's hard to know whether the captain would have spoken Irish or Latin to Patricius; but Patricius, though his Latin is abysmally awkward at times, has a good ear for dialogue. Here is the original, which gives us an excellent idea of how ordinary men used the tongue of Cicero: *"Quid est, Christiane? Tu dicis deus tuus magnus et omnipotens est; quare ergo non potes pro nobis orare? Quia nos a fame periclitamur; difficile est enim ut aliquem hominem umquam videamus!"*

"From the bottom of your heart, turn trustingly to the Lord my God," the visionary instructs them, "for nothing is impossible to him. And today he will send you food for your journey until you are filled, for he has an abundance everywhere." The young man's sincerity affects the weakened sailors, who, bowing their heads, try a moment of faith. The sound of a stampede attracts their attention; and as they raise their eyes, a herd of pigs hoofs it down the road in their direction. Not just food, but the best food of all!

It takes him a few more years, but Patricius at last makes it home to Britain, where he is "welcomed as a son" by his parents, who beg him not to go off anywhere and leave them again. (For all the awkwardness of his prose, Patricius can sometimes give us just the right details, as in this portrait of his anxious family.) But Patricius is no longer a carefree Roman teenager. Hardened physically and psychologically by unsharable experiences, hopelessly behind his peers in education, he cannot settle down. One night in his parents' house, a man he knew in Ireland visits him in vision: Victoricus, holding "countless letters," one of which he hands to Patricius, who reads its heading—VOX HIBERIONACUM, The Voice of the Irish. At that moment, he hears the voice of a multitude (beside a forest that Patricius remembers as being "near the western sea"), ✦ crying: "We beg you to come and walk among us once more." "Stabbed in the heart," he is unable to read further —and so wakes up.

Try though he might, he cannot put the Irish out of his mind. The visions increase, and Christ begins

✦ I take the sea to be the Irish Sea—"western" to the Britons who are the audience for P.'s *Confession.* Others, who doubt the tradition surrounding Miliucc (a king in Antrim), place the forest in Mayo and imagine that P. served his time in the west of Ireland. But this is unlikely, given the area of Ireland to which he returned. The Patrician material is full of such difficulties: e.g., the sailors who rescued P. may not have been transporting dogs (it depends on which manuscript you follow)—though they were almost certainly transporting some cargo. Likewise, many think that the "desert" was in Britain and that P.'s party journeyed in one direction for twenty-eight days! The dates of P.'s life and travels are also in dispute. See Bibliographical Sources for additional information.

to speak within him: "He who gave his life for you, he it is who speaks within you." Patricius, the escaped slave, is about to be drafted once more—as Saint Patrick, apostle to the Irish nation.

Patrick will never make up for the formal education he missed while herding sheep in Antrim. His whole life will be shadowed by his ignorance of Latin style, and his consequent inability to communicate with distinguished men on their own level. One sometimes wonders, reading his *Confession* (singular, unlike Augustine's plural), if the poor man even has a language of his own. His mother tongue was possibly an early form of Welsh, though it is just as likely that, as in Augustine's house, the "native" tongue was for the servants and only Latin was spoken by the family. He missed all but elementary Latin schooling—and then was plunged into a new language: Irish, similar in certain ways to Welsh, but even at this period markedly different.

When he can hold out no longer, he leaves his family once more and follows his voices to Gaul—probably to the island monastery of Lérins, just offshore from present-day Cannes, where he petitions for a theological education in preparation for ordination. Patrick is no complainer, so we can only imagine what this course of studies took out of him and how often he may have wished for the chill and hunger of Antrim in preference to the torturous drudgery of studies for which he was so ill prepared. The night before his ordination as deacon, he confides to a friend a rankling sin that he committed at fifteen, and receives forgiveness. At this period, as through much of Christian history, "confession" meant a declaration of the state of one's soul, made publicly—or, as was becoming more common, to a friend, who could then confirm God's forgiveness. This private confession would come back to haunt Patrick in his age.

At length, he is ordained priest and bishop, virtually the first missionary bishop in history. We understand that Jesus's apostles preached his Good News—Good Spell or Gospel, to use the Old English term—after the descent of the Spirit at the Feast of Pentecost in Jerusalem and that they intended to preach "to the ends of the earth." We are a little uncertain as to how far most of them actually got, though we think Peter was nailed upside down to a cross at Rome. Thomas—in legend, at least— got as far as India. But the first Christian missionary for whom we have extensive documentation is Paul, not one of the original apostles, but an apostle, as he puts it, "appointed not by human beings"—that is, appointed by vision. Patrick may be the second such appointment. What is remarkable is not that Patrick should have felt an overwhelming sense of mission but that in the four centuries between Paul and Patrick there are no missionaries.

To Roman citizens, the place to be was a Roman city or villa. The *pagus,* the uncultivated countryside, inevitably suggested discomfort and hardship. The inhabitants of the *pagus— pagani,* or pagans—were country bumpkins, rustic, unreliable, threatening. Roman Christians assumed this prejudice without examining it. Augustine, in his profundity, realized that the ahistorical Platonic ascent to Wisdom through knowledge and leisured contemplation was unaccomplishable and that it must be replaced by the biblical journey through time—through the life of each man and through the life of the race. Still, the words *iter* (journey) and *peregrinatio* (pilgrimage) made him shudder.

As bishop of Hippo, he almost never visited the country districts over which he held nominal sway, and once when he did he was nearly ambushed by Circumcellions, radical Donatists who were a sort of Christian combination of Act Up and the Party of God. His travels to Rome and Milan as a young man were never repeated, nor would he in a million years have thought of venturing beyond the Ecumene—the territory under Roman governance. Beyond the Ecumene, outside the Imperium, lay chaos unimaginable: "Here do be monsters," the medieval maps would say of unmapped territory.

In truth, even Paul, the great missionary apostle, though he endured all the miseries of classical travel for the sake of the Gospel, never himself ventured beyond the Greco-Roman Ecumene. Thomas, presumed apostle to India, though traveling perhaps beyond the official Ecumene, would have proselytized an ancient civilization with many ties to the Greek world. So Patrick was really a first—the first missionary to barbarians beyond the reach of Roman law. The step he took was in its way as bold as Columbus's, and a thousand times more humane. He himself was aware of its radical nature. "The Gospel," he reminded his accusers late in his life, "has been preached to the point beyond which there is no one"—nothing but the ocean. Nor was he blind to his dangers, for even in his last years "every day I am ready to be murdered, betrayed, enslaved—whatever may come my way. But I am not afraid of any of these things, because of the promises of heaven; for I have put myself in the hands of God Almighty."

Saint Patrick was a gentleman,
And he came from *dacent* people,

goes a music hall ditty of the nineteenth century. He did, indeed. And he was a good and brave man, one of humanity's natural noblemen. Among simple, straightforward people, who could unreservedly appreciate his core of decency, the success of his mission was assured.

His love for his adopted people shines through his writings, and it is not just a generalized "Christian" benevolence, but a love for individuals as they are. He tells us of "a blessed woman, Irish by birth, noble, extraordinarily beautiful *(pulcherrima)*—a true adult—whom I baptized." Who could imagine such frank admiration of a woman from the pen of Augustine? Who could imagine such particularity of observation from most of those listed in the calendar of saints?

He worries constantly for his people, not just for their spiritual but for their physical welfare. The horror of slavery was never lost on him: "But it is the women kept in slavery who suffer the most—and who keep their spirits up despite the menacing and terrorizing they must endure. The Lord gives grace to his many handmaids; and though they are forbidden to do so, they follow him with backbone." Patrick has become an Irishman, a man who can give far more credibility to a woman's strength and fortitude than could any classically educated man.

In his last years, he could probably look out over an Ireland transformed by his teaching. According to tradition, at least, he established bishops throughout northern, central, and eastern Ireland: he is primatial bishop at Ard Macha (modern Armagh), a hill away from Emain Macha, seat of the Ulster kings descended from Derdriu's persecutor, Conchobor; and he has set up a bishop close by Tara, home of the high king (chosen—in theory, by rotation!—from among the provincial kings), and beside the capitals of the kings of northern and southern Leinster. He has even created a bishopric as far west as Cruachan, Medb's ancient capital of Connacht, though Munster in the south will remain pagan for a generation more. The practice of associating bishoprics with local kingships Patrick took no doubt from the continental model of church organization. But whereas Augustine might have viewed this arrangement as ideal for currying favor and subtly and gradually increasing the power of the church, Patrick could have had no such motives. For ancient Ireland had no *civitates,* no population centers of any kind—just scattered and isolated farmsteads. By placing his bishops next door to the kings, Patrick hoped to keep an eye on the most powerful raiders and rustlers and limit their depredations.

With the Irish—even with the kings—he succeeded beyond measure. Within his lifetime or soon after his death, the Irish slave trade came to a halt, and other forms of violence, such as murder and intertribal warfare, decreased. In reforming Irish sexual mores, he was rather less successful, though he established indigenous monasteries and convents, whose inmates by their way of life reminded the Irish that the virtues of lifelong faithfulness, courage, and generosity were actually attainable by ordinary human beings and that the sword was not the only instrument for structuring a society.

Patrick's relations with his British brothers were less happy. Rising petty kings along the western coasts of Britain, rushing to fill the power vacuum left by the departure of the Roman legions, began to carve out new territories for themselves and to take up piracy, an activity the Christian Britons had long ago abandoned. The forces of one of these kings, Coroticus, de-

Ireland in the early fifth century

scended on the now peaceful coast of northern Ireland and, butchering many and seizing booty, carted off Patrick's converts in the thousands—"the chrism still fragrant on their foreheads," describes the outraged apostle.

He sends a delegation of priests to the court of Coroticus in the hopes of ransoming the captives, but when they get there they are laughed to scorn. Having failed to gain a hearing from the king and now at his wit's end, Patrick writes an open letter to British Christians in an attempt to put pressure on Coroticus. It is a wail of mourning for his lost people: "Patricide, fratricide! ravening wolves eating up the people of the Lord as it were bread! . . . I beseech you earnestly, it is not right to pay court to such men nor to take food and drink in their company, nor is it right to accept their alms, until they by doing strict penance with shedding of tears make amends before God and free the servants of God and the baptized handmaids of Christ for whom he was crucified and died."

When he writes of this "crime so horrible and unspeakable," Patrick's ardor is fueled, of course, by the memory of his own horrible experiences. In this period of human development, only a former slave could have condemned the slave trade with such heat. The mention of alms alerts us that the correspondents on whom Patrick hopes to have the greatest effect are the British bishops—which is also why he alludes constantly to his people's baptism. If these bishops will bestir themselves and excommunicate Coroticus, it will only be a matter of time before a well-organized conspiracy of social isolation will break the king's resolve.

We don't know if Patrick's ploy was successful. But we do know that, even in the midst of his agony, he saw clearly the obstacle to his success: "In sadness and grief, shall I cry aloud. O most lovely and loving brethren and sons whom I have begotten in Christ (I cannot number them), what shall I do for you? I am not worthy to come to the aid of either God or men. The wickedness of the wicked has prevailed against us. We are become as it were strangers. Can it be that they do not believe that we have received one baptism or that we have one God and Father? Is it a shameful thing in their eyes that we have been born in Ireland?"

The British Christians did not recognize the Irish Christians either as full-fledged Christians or as human beings—because they were not Roman. Patrick, whose awkward foreignness on his return to Britain had been the cause of numerous rebuffs, knows in his bones the snobbery of the educated Roman, who by the mid-fifth century had every right to assume that Roman and Christian were interchangeable identities. Patrick, operating at the margins of European geography and of human consciousness, has traveled even further from his birthright than we might expect. He is no longer British or Roman, at all. When he cries out in his pain, "Is it a shameful thing . . . that *we* have been born in Ireland?" we know that he has left the old civilization behind forever and has identified himself completely with the Irish.

His British brothers find his conduct inexplicable, and they look for some ulterior motive. He went to Ireland to con riches from the guileless Irish—haven't you heard that he charges for baptisms and bishoprics? Did you know that he was a swineherd to begin with, a filthy little pigkeeper? Did you know— it's quite a scandal, really, almost cost him his ordination—did you know that in his youth he . . . ? Against such vicious whisperings, Patrick writes his plainspoken *Confession,* defending his life of service in the face of the publicly expressed doubts of those he calls *"dominicati rhetorici"*—the classically trained priests of Britain, the clerical intelligentsia. Somehow, even the private confession he had made on the eve of his ordination has become grist for their mill, and the sin he had confessed then has become current gossip.

My guess is that the sin was murder. He was fifteen—and how many sins are available to a fifteen-year-old that would still bother him by midlife, especially after a life as various and harsh as Patrick's? (Patrick committed the sin in, let us say, 400, was kidnapped the following year and escaped perhaps in 407, but was not ordained till about 430, since he did not return to Ireland till about 432, when he would have been—at least, according to this reckoning—forty-seven.) Despite Augustine's later preoccupations, sexual sins were not high on most people's lists in those days. Theft on a grand scale would have been even more unlikely, given his family's atmosphere and attentiveness. But murder, especially of a slave or servant, would have borne no social consequences—nor would it have meant much to the murderer until he found himself at the receiving end of someone else's brutality. In any case, the ferocity of this normally placid, quiet man courses to the surface only when slavery or human carnage is the subject.

However blind his British contemporaries may have been to it, the greatness of Patrick is beyond dispute: the first human being in the history of the world to speak out unequivocally against slavery. Nor will any voice as strong as his be heard again till the seventeenth century. In his own time, only the Irish appreciated him for who he was; beyond their borders he was as little known as Augustine was in Ireland. Patrick himself probably never heard of Augustine, who died two years before Patrick set sail as bishop; and if he did hear of him he undoubtedly never read him. In those days, news could take a year to travel from one end of the crumbling empire to the other; books could take a decade or two—or even half a century. But Patrick shows us that he understood the dual concept of the City of Man and the City of God as well as Augustine himself when he derides Coroticus and his men as "dogs and sorcerers and murderers, and liars and false swearers . . . who distribute baptized girls for a price, and that for the sake of a miserable temporal kingdom which truly passes away in a moment like a cloud or smoke that is scattered by the wind." But of his beloved, slaughtered warrior children: "O most dear ones . . . I can see you, beginning the journey to the land where there is no night nor sorrow nor death. . . . You shall reign with the apostles and prophets and martyrs. You shall seize the everlasting kingdoms, as he himself promised, when he said: 'They shall come from the east and the west and shall sit down with Abraham and Isaac and Jacob in the kingdom of heaven.' "

Patrick's emotional grasp of Christian truth may have been greater than Augustine's. Augustine looked into his own heart and found there the inexpressible anguish of each individual, which enabled him to articulate a theory of sin that has no equal—the dark side of Christianity. Patrick prayed, made peace with God, and then looked not only into his own heart but into the hearts of others. What he saw convinced him of the bright side—that even slave traders can turn into liberators, even murderers can act as peacemakers, even barbarians can take their places among the nobility of heaven.

In becoming an Irishman, Patrick wedded his world to theirs, his faith to their life. For Augustine and the Roman church of the first five centuries, baptism, the mystical water ceremony in which the naked catechumen dies to sin, was the foundation of a Christian life. Patrick found a way of swimming down to the depths of the Irish psyche and warming and transforming Irish imagination—making it more humane and more noble while keeping it Irish. No longer would baptismal water be the only effective sign of a new life in God. New life was everywhere in rank abundance, and all of God's creation was good. The druids, the pagan Irish priests who claimed to be able to control the elements, felt threatened by Patrick, who knew that a humble prayer could even make food materialize in a barren desert—because all the world was the work of his Creator-God.

Of the many legends surrounding Patrick, few can be authenticated. He did not chase the snakes out of Ireland. There is no way of knowing whether he used the shamrock to explain the Trinity. He probably did have a confrontation with a king, possibly the high king at Tara, and it may have been over his right to commemorate Christ's resurrection by lighting a bonfire—the same fire that has become a permanent feature of all Easter liturgies. Even Patrick's great prayer in Irish—sometimes called "Saint Patrick's Breastplate" because it was thought to protect him from hostile powers, sometimes called "The Deer's Cry" because it was thought to make him resemble a deer to the eyes of those seeking to do him harm—cannot be definitely ascribed to him. Characteristics of its language would assign it to the seventh, or even to the eighth, century. On the other hand, it is Patrician to its core, the first ringing assertion that the universe itself is the Great Sacrament, magically designed by its loving Creator to bless and succor human beings. The earliest expression of European vernacular poetry, it is, in attitude, the work of a Christian druid, a man of both faith and magic. Its feeling is entirely un-Augustinian; but it is this feeling that will go on to animate the best poetry of the Middle Ages. If Patrick did not write it (at least in its current form), it surely takes its inspiration from him. For in this cosmic incantation, the inarticulate outcast who wept for slaves, aided common men in difficulty, and loved sunrise and sea at last finds his voice. Appropriately, it is an Irish voice:

I arise today
Through a mighty strength, the invocation of the Trinity,
Through belief in the threeness,
Through confession of the oneness
Of the Creator of Creation.

I arise today
Through the strength of Christ's birth with his baptism,

Through the strength of his crucifixion with his burial,
Through the strength of his resurrection with his ascension,
Through the strength of his descent for the judgment of
    Doom.

I arise today
Through the strength of the love of Cherubim,
In obedience of angels,
In the service of archangels,
In hope of resurrection to meet with reward,
In prayers of patriarchs,
In predictions of prophets,
In preaching of apostles,
In faith of confessors,
In innocence of holy virgins,
In deeds of righteous men.

I arise today
Through the strength of heaven:
Light of sun,
Radiance of moon,
Splendor of fire,
Speed of lightning,
Swiftness of wind,
Depth of sea,
Stability of earth,
Firmness of rock.

I arise today
Through God's strength to pilot me:
God's might to uphold me,

God's wisdom to guide me,
God's eye to look before me,
God's ear to hear me,
God's word to speak for me,
God's hand to guard me,
God's way to lie before me,
God's shield to protect me,
God's host to save me
From snares of devils,
From temptations of vices,
From everyone who shall wish me ill,
Afar and anear,
Alone and in multitude.

I summon today all these powers between me and those
    evils,
Against every cruel merciless power that may oppose my
    body and soul
Against incantations of false prophets,
Against black laws of pagandom,
Against false laws of heretics,
Against craft of idolatry, ·
Against spells of witches and smiths and wizards,
Against every knowledge that corrupts man's body and soul.

Christ to shield me today
Against poison, against burning,
Against drowning, against wounding,
So that there may come to me abundance of reward.
Christ with me, Christ before me, Christ behind me,
Christ in me, Christ beneath me, Christ above me,

Christ on my right, Christ on my left,
Christ when I lie down, Christ when I sit down, Christ
  when I arise,
Christ in the heart of every man who thinks of me,
Christ in the mouth of everyone who speaks of me,
Christ in every eye that sees me,
Christ in every ear that hears me.

I arise today
Through a mighty strength, the invocation of the Trinity,
Through belief in the threeness,
Through confession of the oneness,
Of the Creator of Creation.

V

A Solid
World
of
Light

Holy Ireland

Patrick devoted the last thirty years of his life—from, roughly, his late forties to his late seventies—to his warrior children, that they might "seize the everlasting kingdoms" with all the energy and intensity they had lately devoted to killing and enslaving one another and seizing one another's kingdoms. When he used that phrase in his open letter to the British Christians, he was echoing the mysterious saying of Jesus, which seems almost to have been uttered with the Irish in mind: "From the days of John the Baptist until now, the kingdom of heaven suffereth violence, and the violent bear it away."◆ In the Gospel story, the passionate, the outsized, the out-of-control have a better shot at seizing heaven than the contained, the calculating, and those of whom this world approves. Patrick, indeed, seems to have been attracted to the same kinds of oddball, off-center personalities that attracted Jesus, and this attraction alone makes him unusual in the history of churchmen.

This thirty-year span of Patrick's mission in the middle of the fifth century encompasses a period of change so rapid and extreme that Europe will never see its like again. By 461, the likely year of Patrick's death, the Roman Empire is careening in chaos, barely fifteen years away from the death of the last western emperor. The accelerated

◆ The phrase "the violent bear it away" fascinated the twentieth-century Irish-American storyteller Flannery O'Connor, who used it as the title of one of her novels. O'Connor's surname connects her to an Irish royal family descended from Conchobor (pronounced "Connor"), the prehistoric king of Ulster who was foster father to Cuchulainn and "husband" of the unwilling Derdriu. In the western world, the antiquity of Irish lineages is exceeded only by that of the Jews.

change is, at this point, so dramatic we should not be surprised that the eyes of historians have been riveted on it or that they have failed to notice a transformation just as dramatic—and even more abrupt—taking place at the empire's periphery. For as the Roman lands went from peace to chaos, the land of Ireland was rushing even more rapidly from chaos to peace.

How did Patrick do it? We have noted already his earthiness and warmth. But these are qualities that make for a lowering of hostility and suspicion; of themselves they do not gain converts among the strong-willed. We can also be sure that the Irish found Patrick admirable according to their own highest standards: his courage—his refusal to be afraid of *them*—would have impressed them immediately; and, as his mission lengthened into years and came to be seen clearly as a lifetime commitment, his steadfast loyalty and supernatural generosity must have moved them deeply. For he had transmuted their pagan virtues of loyalty, courage, and generosity into the Christian equivalents of faith, hope, and charity. But, though this singular display of virtue would have made friends, it would not necessarily have won converts—at least, not among a people as stubborn as the Irish.

Throughout the Roman world, Christianity had accompanied Romanization. Its spread through the empire cannot be understood apart from Romanization. Just as the subject peoples had wanted to be Roman, they came quickly to understand that they wanted to be Christian, too. From the fourth century on, instruction in Christianity could even serve as a shortcut to Romanization, as joining the Episcopalians was till recently a shortcut to respectability in America. Once the emperor had conferred on Christianity its position of privilege,

The Roman Empire in the early fifth century

most Romans had little difficulty in reading this sign of the times for what it was and grasping that their own best interest lay in church membership. Though it would be cynical and ahistorical to conclude that conversions to Christianity in late antiquity were made only for the sake of political advancement or social convenience, it would be naive to imagine that Christianity swept the empire only because of its evident spiritual superiority. Certainly, the Christians of the first three centuries, whose adherence to Christianity could easily prove their death warrant, were devout and extraordinary. But from the time of Constantine, the vast majority of Christian converts were fairly superficial people. Despite Augustine's enormous influence on subsequent history, the bland, detached, calculating Ausonius was a far more typical Christian of the late empire than was the earnest bishop of Hippo.

Patrick, unable to offer worldly improvement to prospective converts, had to find a way of connecting his message to their deepest concerns. It was a challenge no one had had to face since the days when Christianity was new and women and slaves had flocked to it as a way of life that raised their status and dignity as human beings. In order to rediscover the amazing connection that Patrick made between the Gospel story and Irish life, we need to delve deeper into the consciousness of the Irish people at this singular hinge in their history.

Their consciousness—and, maybe even more important, their subconscious. For in the dreams of a people, if we can read these aright, lie their most profound fears and their most exalted aspirations. We know something of Irish dreams, for we can piece together their mythology—their collective dream-story—from the oral tales of the pre-Christian period (such as the *Tain*) that were subsequently written down and from the artifacts uncovered by archaeologists. Since neither the tales nor the artifacts can offer us a whole mythology—the complete Irish dream cycle—we must read these materials as if they were the fragments of a great papyrus.

It would be understatement to assert that the Irish gods were not the friendliest of figures. Actually, there are few idols that we have retrieved from barrow or bog that would not give a child nightmares and an adult the willies. No smooth-skinned, well-proportioned Apollos and Aphrodites here. Archaeological finds at Celtic sites beyond Ireland serve only to underscore the monstrousness of the Celtic pantheon, as do the few appearances of gods in the *Tain*. When, for instance, the warriors of Connacht bivouac on their way to Cuailnge, the druid Dubthach chants a prophecy while they eat their evening meal. The vision that he conjures up, though deliberately obscure, is of an impending battle, one that will end with "man's meat everywhere"—a phrase that can hardly have improved the digestion of the troops. As they sleep, the war goddess "Nemain assailed them. They had no peace that night, with their sleep broken by Dubthach's brute outcry. Groups of them started up, and many of the army remained troubled until Medb came and calmed them."

Medb is herself a kind of goddess. Her name is a cognate of the English word *mead* and may be found as a root in many Indo-European languages, meaning something like "she who intoxicates"—which was probably how she reduced the troops to slumber. Insensate drunkenness was the warrior's customary prelude to sleep.

On the night before the last battle between Connacht and Ulster, a sinister shape-changing goddess called the Morrigan spoke "in the half light between the two camps," describing in gory detail all the horrors of the morrow. That night two war goddesses, Nemain and Badb, "called out to the men of Ireland near the field at Gairech and Irgairech, and a hundred warriors died of fright. It was a bad night for them," concludes the storyteller with compact understatement.

So, an obscure prophecy could banish sleep that only excessive drink could restore, and a dim flickering in the twilight or a cry in the night could kill a hundred men. Beneath the bravado of this warrior society, constantly brandishing its flesh-destroying weapons, rumbles a quaking fear so acute that it can kill. The conscious indifference to death that is a hallmark of all the heroes of the *Táin* masks a subconscious fear of death that no public rhetoric can erase.

Patrick held out to these warrior children, in his own person, a living alternative. It is possible to be brave—to expect "every day . . . to be murdered, betrayed, enslaved—whatever may come my way"—and yet be a man of peace and at peace, a man without sword or desire to harm, a man in whom the sharp fear of death has been smoothed away. He was "not afraid of any of these things, because of the promises of heaven; for I have put myself in the hands of God Almighty." Patrick's peace was no sham: it issued from his person like a fragrance. And in a damp land where people lived and slept in close proximity, everyone would have known sooner or later if Patrick's sleep was brought on by the goddess of intoxication or broken by the goddesses of fear. Patrick slept soundly and soberly.

Just as there was in the Irish psyche a cleft between conscious bravery and unconscious fear, so we can also discern other conscious-subconscious dualities that give us excellent clues to the true temper of this race of seemingly carefree warriors. In virtually all the Irish tales, for instance, we come upon the Celtic phenomenon of shape-shifting, an effect that the Irish seem to have taken for granted as we take for granted molecular structures: this was simply the way the world was. Shape-shifting was the ability of a being to turn itself into something else, and it went far beyond the metamorphosis of the warp-spasm. We have already seen a splendid example of shape-shifting in Amhairghin's foundation lyric: he is first an estuary, then a wave, then the pounding of the sea, then an ox, then a hawk, and so on. And though a contemporary reader might take all this as metaphor, the Irish believed that gods, druids, poets, and others in touch with the magical world could be literal shape-shifters. In *The Voyage of Bran, Son of Febal, to the Land of the Living,* the wizard Tuan Mac Cairill, celebrates his protean life:

A hawk to-day, a boar yesterday,
Wonderful instability! . . .

Among herds of boars I was,
Though to-day I am among bird-flocks;
I know what will come of it:
I shall still be in another shape!

But however wonderful this instability may have seemed to the conscious Irish imagination, it had its dark side as well, for it suggested subconsciously that reality had no predictable pattern, but was arbitrary and insubstantial. There is within this worldview a terrifying personal implication: that I myself have no fixed identity but am, like the rest of reality, essentially fluid —essentially inessential. Of course, the Irish had no way of expressing such ideas directly. One needs a sense of identity before one can complain of its absence. But this wonderful and terrifying instability haunts virtually every sentence of the ancient literature.

Allied to their experience of reality's fluidity is their understanding that the world is full of hidden traps, as if it were a forest filled with concealed pitfalls by which hunter-gods catch small animals. In another story, *The Destruction of Da Derga's*

Hostel, the hero Conaire, whose bird-man father was a shape-shifter, is warned against hunting birds by a bird who changes into a man and announces that he is "Nemglan, king of your father's birds." Nemglan tells Conaire that he must go to Tara, for he is to be high king, but that during his reign

> birds shall be privileged, and this shall be your observance always: you shall not pass Tara on your right hand and Bregia on your left; you shall not hunt the crooked beasts of Cerna; and you shall not stay abroad from Tara for nine nights; and you shall not spend the night in a house from which firelight is visible outside after sunset and into which one can see from outside; and three red-haired men shall not go before you into a red-haired man's house; and plunder shall not be taken during your reign; the visit of one woman shall not come into your house after sunset; and you shall not settle a quarrel between two of your subjects.

In short, Conaire's reign is doomed, for there is no way he can successfully respect all these taboos. Indeed, hostile powers trigger the violation of each taboo in turn, thus precipitating Conaire's inevitable downfall.

There is not a hero in ancient Irish literature who does not fall prey to some taboo or another—*geis,* the Irish called it *(gessa* in the plural), a word that may perhaps be translated as "observance." We are familiar with such Iron Age observances from the land mines and booby traps of the Greek myths: Achilles's heel, his one bit of vulnerability, is what proves fatal to him; Oedipus's prophesied fate—that he will murder his father and sleep with his mother—turns out to be inescapable, though he does everything he can to avoid it. But in the Irish stories the traps seem to lie hidden at every crossroads, and trickster-gods lurk behind each tree. In such a world, where no one can hope to avoid disaster for long, the boy Cuchulainn's choice of a short life and eternal fame makes perfect sense. Once more, the cold-eyed truth in the face of the Dying Gaul appears before us.

Patrick could put himself—imaginatively—in the position of the Irish. To him, no less than to them, the world is full of magic. One can invoke the elements—the lights of heaven, the waves of the sea, the birds and the animals—and these will come to one's aid, as in the incantation of the "Breastplate." The difference between Patrick's magic and the magic of the druids is that in Patrick's world all beings and events come from the hand of a good God, who loves human beings and wishes them success. And though that success is of an ultimate kind—and, therefore, does not preclude suffering—all nature, indeed the whole of the created universe, conspires to mankind's good, teaching, succoring, and saving.

Patrick could speak convincingly of these things. He could assure you that all suffering, however dull and desperate, would come to its conclusion and would show itself to have been worthwhile. He could insist that, in the end, you too would hear the words "Your hungers are rewarded: you are going home. Look, your ship is ready." He could speak believably of the superabundance of a God who in response to humble prayer feeds his lost and wandering people with heavenly manna—and a crew of lost and starving sailors with a herd of very earthly pigs. For Patrick, as for the nineteenth-century mystical poet Gerard Manley Hopkins, who was also deeply influenced by Celtic sensibility,

The world is charged with the grandeur of God.
It will flame out, like shining from shook foil—

just as do the cunning little birds and charmingly complicated animals of Celtic metalwork.

The key to Patrick's confidence—and it is the sort of ringing, rock-solid confidence on which a civilization may be built, an unmuffled confidence not heard since the Golden Ages of Greece and Rome—is in his reliance on "the Creator of Creation," the phrase with which the "Breastplate" opens and closes. Our Father in heaven, having created all things, even things that have since become bent or gone bad, will deliver us, his children, from all evil. But our Father is not only in faraway heaven, but lives among us. For he created everything by his Word, which was with him in the beginning, which became flesh in the human Jesus, and flames out in all his creatures:

I see his blood upon the rose
And in the stars the glory of his eyes,
His body gleams amid eternal snows,
His tears fall from the skies.

I see his face in every flower;
The thunder and the singing of the birds
Are but his voice—and carven by his power
Rocks are his written words.

All pathways by his feet are worn,
His strong heart stirs the ever-beating sea,

His crown of thorns is twined with every thorn,
His cross is every tree.

This magical world, though full of adventure and surprise, is no longer full of dread. Rather, Christ has trodden all pathways before us, and at every crossroads and by every tree the Word of God speaks out. We have only to be quiet and listen, as Patrick learned to do during the silence of his "novitiate" as a shepherd on the slopes of Sliabh Mis.

This sense of the world as holy, as the Book of God—as a healing mystery, fraught with divine messages—could never have risen out of Greco-Roman civilization, threaded with the profound pessimism of the ancients and their Platonic suspicion of the body as unholy and the world as devoid of meaning. Even Augustine, whose synthesis of pagan and Christian attitudes is the most remarkable philosophical creation of Christianity's first five centuries, can come nowhere near Patrick's originality. True, Augustine's theories on sin will haunt the Middle Ages, and cast their shadows still. But from the celebratory spirit of the "Breastplate" will spring the characteristic art and poetry of the western world—the immense symbolic power of the medieval liturgy, the smiling angels of Gothic art, the laughable demons, the sweetness of poets like Francis of Assisi (whose "Canticle of the Sun" could almost be mistaken for a Celtic poem), Dante (who spoke of "the love that moves the sun and the other stars"), and Chaucer (whose "Crea*tour* of every crea*ture*" is almost a line from the "Breastplate"). Nor did this spirit die at the close of the Middle Ages. For it remains a continuing tradition in British and Irish poetry that takes us down to the present—from the gentle visions of George Herbert and Thomas Traherne to the excited ecstasies of Gerard Manley Hopkins, from the mysticism of Joseph Plunkett—who wrote "I See His Blood upon the Rose" not in the fifth century but in the twentieth**—to the Christian druidism of Seamus Heaney, who to this day is carving out poems that might stop even Derdriu in her tracks.

In this tradition, there is a trust in the objects of sensory perception, which are seen as signposts from God. But there is also a sensuous reveling in the splendors of the created world, which would have made Roman Christians exceedingly uncomfortable. I think it likely that, had Augustine ever read the "Breastplate," he would have sniffed heresy. Even in Patrick's *Confession* and *Letter,* which no one disputes came from his pen, there are emphases and omissions that Augustine would have found unnerving. Where, in Patrick's own story, is there any negative treatment of the temptations of the flesh? Aside from the ambiguous incident in which the sailors offer their nipples to be sucked, the only passages that come anywhere near the subject of sex are Patrick's notice of the "most beautiful" Irish princess, whom he baptizes, and his horror that his female converts have been made into sex slaves by the soldiers of Coroticus. Patrick is as silent about sex as are the Gospels.

It may simply be that Patrick, in his zeal to baptize—to wash clean—Irish imagination, was not as sex-obsessed as his continental brethren and felt little need to stress these matters. Before his mission, Irish

** Plunkett, a visionary poet from a noble Irish house and lateral descendant of the Elizabethan martyr and archbishop of Armagh Oliver Plunkett, was executed by the British in 1916 for his part in the Easter Rising. A very different poet, Edith Sitwell, wrote a comparable poem later in the century, "Still Falls the Rain," in which she imagines the incessant rain during an air raid in 1940 as the mercy of Christ.

sexual arrangements were relatively improvisational. Trial "marriages" of one year, multiple partners, and homosexual relations among warriors on campaign were all more or less the order of the day. Despite Patrick's great success in changing the warrior mores of the Irish tribes, their sexual mores altered little. Even the monasteries he established were not especially notable for their rigid devotion to the rule of chastity; and as late as the end of the twelfth century Geraldus Cambrensis reports that the kings of Clan Conaill continue to be inaugurated in the high style of their ancestors—by public copulation with a white mare.

None of this should be surprising if we assume that there were characteristic aspects of Irish civilization that Patrick had taken to heart and on which he chose to build his new Christianity. These aspects would have included Irish courage, which he admired greatly, but even more would he have been impressed by the natural mysticism of the Irish, which already told them that the world was holy—all the world, not just parts of it. It was on this sturdy insight that Patrick choreographed the sacred dance of Irish sacramental life, a sacramentality not limited to the symbolic actions of the church's liturgy but open to the whole created universe. All the world was holy, and so was all the body.

Patrick's adventures in the Irish dreamworld must have reached their crucial moment when he faced the phenomenon of human sacrifice. All early peoples sacrificed human beings. One has only to remember Agamemnon's sacrifice to angry Artemis of the most beautiful thing he possessed, his daughter Iphigenia. But this was a story of the Greek Iron Age, no more present to the Romanized world into which Patrick was born than public executions are to ours. For us, it is a strain to find *any* surviving elements of sacrifice—cut flowers, Christmas trees, vigil lights, and the Mass may be the last vestiges—but in the Roman world animal sacrifices were still offered. These were scarcely different from the animal sacrifices we read of in the Jewish scriptures, sacrifices that were still being offered in the temple as Jesus was led to Calvary and the blood of newborn lambs darkened the river that flowed through Jerusalem.

It seems that at some point in the development of every culture, human sacrifice becomes unthinkable, and animals are from then on substituted for human victims. The story of the Binding of Isaac in Genesis may constitute symbolically just such a turning point in the history of the Jews—when Abraham's God tells him it is no longer required that he sacrifice his only son, but may substitute a ram instead. At all events, the Irish had not reached this point and were still sacrificing human beings to their gods when Patrick began his mission. They sacrificed prisoners of war to the war gods and newborns to the harvest gods. Believing that the human head was the seat of the soul, they displayed proudly the heads of their enemies in their temples and on their palisades; they even hung them from their belts as ornaments, used them as footballs in victory celebrations, and were fond of employing skull tops as ceremonial drinking bowls. They also sculpted heads—both shrunken, decapitated heads and overbearing, impassive godheads—and a favorite motif was the head of a tri-faced god, for three was their magical number, and gods and goddesses often manifested themselves as three.

Why do human beings do these things? The psychological mechanism is not far to find, since there is probably not a reader—even the most convinced atheist—who has not offered from time to time an old-fashioned *quid pro quo* prayer: if you let me pass this exam, I will return to church; if you make sure my wife doesn't learn of my infidelity, I will give my next bonus to charity. The theology—the view of god—that lies behind these imprecations is of an arbitrary trickster, a bad parent who can be coaxed, flattered, and manipulated. If belief in such a god is strong and primitive enough, it is easy to see how it can lead to human sacrifice: *Here, take him, not me!* The impassive godhead demands someone's blood. *Let it not be mine!* I am not sure that some of our more inexplicable murders—the victims of Jeffrey Dahmer in Milwaukee, the small child killed by two other children in Liverpool—are not explained best by this prehistoric impulse. Certainly, the most appalling of war crimes, such as those being perpetrated in the bloody tragedies of Bosnia and Rwanda, are human responses to this subterranean prompting. And if we study the faces of the Celtic gods, we can have no doubt that only blood could satisfy most of them.

But we delude ourselves about the complex history of religious feeling if we think that all sacrifice—human included—can be reduced to this base motive. Throughout history, different civilizations have thought very different thoughts—for example, the Greeks thought the cosmos was eternal, whereas we suspect it had a beginning; the Jewish patriarchs never thought of a soul, which was central to Greek thought. But unlike human thought, human *feeling*—like the human body—has not changed at all. Whatever the Irish felt, we feel. For all the terror of the Celtic cosmos and the bloodthirstiness of the Celtic gods, no human society could hold together for long if it understood sacrifice only along the lines of the savage tribe in *King Kong,* offering terrified beauties to the Beast.

This caricature is belied by the most direct evidence of

human sacrifice that we have found to date—the prehistoric corpses of Tolland Man, Grauballe Man, and Borremose Man, dug out of Danish bogs in the 1950s, and an even more intriguing discovery recently made in a remote English bog. The Danish bodies may be Celtic; the English one—a man discovered in 1984 and dug out of the peat of Lindow Moss, an ancient bog south of Manchester—certainly is, and may even be Irish. These bodies all owe their amazing state of preservation to the chemical properties of the peat, which has leatherized the skin but left it otherwise intact, so that we can see every physical detail—even smile lines around the eyes—just as we could have in life. All the bodies were sacrificed, and all the faces are at peace. In other words, all went willingly, one might almost say happily, to their sacrificial deaths—like Isaac, trusting to the last in the goodness of the sacrificing priest and, even more important, in the goodness of the father god.

Like religion in our own day, the Irish religious impulse must have manifested itself in two very different ways. The basely religious would have been glad to sacrifice others to gods they conceived of as ravening horrors, projections of their own psyches and their own twisted lives. These we still find today among religious types who rigidly put principle before people, whose icons (within Christianity) are likely to be bland, breastless madonnas or glassy-eyed Nordic Christs. At the other pole were people like Lindow Man, who willingly died for his people. Between these poles, I'd say, stood the vast majority of Irish votaries, sometimes giving in to their baser religious instincts, sometimes inspired by the nobler ideals of their religion.

That Lindow Man was a sacrifice there can be little doubt. His hands are uncalloused, his nails beautifully manicured.

Thus, he was an aristocrat, though, strangely, he cannot have been a warrior, for his body shows no evidence of the scars of battle. Indeed, leaving aside for the moment the marks of his elaborate execution, he appears to be without blemish of any kind. According to British archaeologists Anne Ross and Don Robins, he was a druid prince who had come from Ireland about A.D. 60, as the Romans were asserting their control and expunging druidism. He offered himself as a sacrifice to the gods for the defeat of the Romans. Ross and Robins even think they know his name—Lovernius, the Fox-Man. Certainly, he had dark red hair and a full beard (like a druid, unlike a bushily mustached warrior) and wore around his left forearm a circlet of fox fur, the naked man's only adornment.

The digestive tracts of all these sacrificial victims have been analyzed to see what their last meal might tell us about their circumstances. In the Danish cases, each last meal was a disgusting potpourri, grains mixed with many other (only marginally edible) plants—a stomach-turning, prehistoric granola! The most obvious conclusion to be drawn from this evidence is that the people of each of the Danish victims, enduring famine and close to starvation, were diluting their dwindling cereal supply with anything that would make it last longer. It is easy to understand a victim's willingness to offer his life to the earth goddess so that she might deign to feed his family.

But Irish Lovernius is another matter. His esophagus was found to contain only some bits of blackened hearthcake, a rather odd last meal. Ross and Robins rightly remind us that a scorched or blackened piece of unleavened bread has long served in Celtic communities as a sign of victimhood. As late as this century, boys in remote Scottish hamlets would meet on the moors on May 1, the ancient feast of Beltaine, kindle a bonfire, and divide a cake in equal pieces corresponding to the number of boys. "They daubed charcoal over one of these until it was perfectly black, and placed all the pieces in a hat. Everyone was blindfolded, and drew out a portion. Whoever drew the black piece was the *devoted* person, and was figuratively sacrificed to Baal [the god of the feast of Beltaine]. He had to leap three times through the flames." One can imagine that once upon a time the sacrifice was hardly figurative.

The most conclusive evidence that the bogmen were sacrificed is the story their bodies tell of the manner of their deaths. Each submitted himself naked to an elaborate, ritualized Triple Death. In the case of Lindow Man, for instance, his skull was flattened by three blows of an ax, his throat garroted by a thrice-knotted sinew cord, his blood emptied quickly through the precise slitting of his jugular. Here is the ancient victim of sacrifice, the offering made out of deep human need. Unblemished, raised to die, possibly firstborn, set aside, gift to the god, food of the god, balm for the people, purification, reparation for all—for sins known and unknown, intended and inadvertent. Behold god's lamb, behold him who takes away the sins of all.

Patrick declared that such sacrifices were no longer needed. Christ had died once for all. I'd bet he quoted Paul, his model, who in his letter to the church at Philippi recited this mysterious poem about sacrifice, the oldest Christian hymn of which we have record:

Though he possessed divine estate
He was not jealous to retain
Equality with God.

He cast off his inheritance,
He took the nature of a slave
And walked as Man among men.

He emptied himself to the last
And was obedient to death—
To death upon a cross.

And, therefore, God has raised him up
And God has given him the Name-
Which-is-above-all-names,

That at the name of Jesus all
In heaven high shall bow the knee
And all the earth and depths

And every tongue of men proclaim
That Jesus Christ is LORD—
To the glory of the Father.

Yes, the Irish would have said, here is a story that answers
our deepest needs—and answers them in a way so good that we
could never even have dared dream of it. We can put away our
knives and abandon our altars. These are no longer required.
The God of the Three Faces has given us his own Son, and we
are washed clean in the blood of this lamb. God does not hate
us; he loves us. Greater love than this no man has than that he
should lay down his life for his friends. That is what God's
Word, made flesh, did for us. From now on, we are all sacrifices
—but without the shedding of blood. It is our lives, not our

deaths, that this God wants. But we *are* to be sacrifices, for Paul adds to the hymn this advice to all: "Let this [same] mind be in you, which was also in Christ Jesus."

The Celts have left us two cups—perhaps the two most famous cups in all of history—which beautifully reveal the story of the transformation of Irish imagination from its fearful and unstable pagan origins to its baptized peace. The first cup is the Gundestrup Cauldron, found in a Danish swamp where it was thrown as a votary offering by a Celtic devotee a century or two before Christ. We know it was intended as an offering because it was newly forged and, in accordance with Celtic custom, broken into pieces before it was offered: it was never intended for normal, human use. (All sacrifices, even the communion bread, must be set aside and somehow broken, consumed, or transformed in order to be authentic. This is part of the "logic" of sacrifice.) The Cauldron is a dazzling feat of silversmithing, its panels alive with gods and warriors. Several panels refer to sacrifice, both animal and human. One panel depicts a gigantic cook-god who drops squirming humans into a vat as we might lobsters. Another, though, depicts a horned god—a figure often referred to as Cernunnos, a god found on coins from India to the British Isles—a lord of animals, surrounded by goat, deer, snake, dolphin, and other members of the animal kingdom, as well as by trefoils of plants and flowers. Against the violence of the warriors and the carnivorous, cannibal gods is set this prehistoric Saint Francis, ruling his peaceable kingdom. The image serves almost as a bridge between the angry Celtic gods, demanding sacrifice, and the Christian God, who offers himself.

The other cup is the Ardagh Chalice, found in a Limerick field and dating to the end of the seventh or the beginning of the eighth century—the same period in which the "Breast-plate" reached its final form. It is the most extraordinary metal-work of the early Middle Ages, both barbaric and refined, solid and airy, bold and restrained. Like the Cauldron, it was forged for ritual, but it makes a happier statement about sacrifice, for the God to whom it is dedicated no longer demands that we nourish him and thus become one with his godhead. The transaction has been reversed: he offers himself to us as heavenly nourishment. In this new "economy," we drink the Blood of God, and all become one by partaking of the one cup, the one destiny. The silver Cauldron was made in thanksgiving for some great favor: it was not meant to be seen by human eyes but was made for the sole delight of the swamp god. The silver Chalice, on the other hand, was meant to delight and refresh the humans who drained its mystical contents. Its elegant bal-ance, its delicate gold filigree interlacings, its blue and ruby enamels beckoned from afar. As the communicant approached the Chalice, he could admire more fully its subtle workman-ship; and as he lifted it to his lips, he would be startled to see, debossed in a band beneath the handles, the almost invisible names of the Twelve Apostles. As he drank the wine—at the very moment of communion—he would briefly upturn the base toward heaven and there would flash skyward the Chalice's most thrilling aspect: the intricate underside of its base, meant to be seen by God alone. This secret pleasure connects the Chalice to the Cauldron and to all the pagan ancestors of the Irish. But the pagan act of pleasuring the god is now absorbed completely into the New Imagination and to all that will fol-low. The smith is still a "man of art," a poet or druid, but he is no longer one of those whose evil craft and power Patrick had to protect himself against:

Against craft of idolatry,
Against spells of witches and smiths and wizards,
Against every knowledge that corrupts man's body and soul.

For God's pleasure and man's are reunited, and earth is shot through with flashes of heaven, and the Chalice has become the druidic Christian smith's thanksgiving, his *deo gratias*.

And that is how the Irish became Christians.

Ulhat Ulas
Found

How the Irish Saved
Civilization

Patrick was a hard-bitten man who did not find his life's purpose till his life was half over. He had a temper that could flare dangerously when he perceived an injustice—not against himself but against another, particularly against someone defenseless. But he had the cheerfulness and good humor that humble people often have. He enjoyed this world and its variety of human beings—and he didn't take himself too seriously. He was, in spirit, an Irishman. "Supreme egotism and utter seriousness are necessary for the greatest accomplishment, and these the Irish find hard to sustain; at some point, the instinct to see life in a comic light becomes irresistible, and ambition falls before it." This insight of William V. Shannon's, if applied to Patrick, casts a peculiar illumination on his personality, and even suggests why his real achievements have remained historically obscure. It also puts Patrick at a further remove from his fellow bishop and confessor, the self-obsessed Augustine.

The exchange between Patrick and his adopted people is marvelous to contemplate. In the overheated Irish cultural environment, mystical attitudes toward the world were taken for granted, as they had never been in the cooler, more rational Roman world. Despite its pagan darkness and shifting insubstantiality, this Irish environment was in the end a more comfortable one for the badly educated shepherd boy to whom God spoke directly. His original home in Roman Britain had become an alien place to him. But the Irish gave Patrick more than a home—they gave him a role, a meaning to his life. For only this former slave had the right instincts to impart to the Irish a New Story, one that made new sense of all their old stories and brought them a peace they had never known before.

Patrick's gift to the Irish was his Christianity—the first de-Romanized Christianity in human history, a Christianity without the sociopolitical baggage of the Greco-Roman world, a Christianity that completely inculturated itself into the Irish scene. Through the Edict of Milan, which had legalized the new religion in 313 and made it the new emperor's pet, Christianity had been received into Rome, not Rome into Christianity! Roman culture was little altered by the exchange, and it is arguable that Christianity lost much of its distinctiveness. But in the Patrician exchange, Ireland, lacking the power and implacable traditions of Rome, had been received into Christianity, which transformed Ireland into Something New, something never seen before—a Christian culture, where slavery and human sacrifice became unthinkable, and warfare, though impossible for humans to eradicate, diminished markedly. The Irish, in any case, loved physical combat too much for intertribal warfare to disappear entirely. But new laws, influenced by Gospel norms, inhibited such conflicts severely by requiring that arms be taken up only for a weighty cause. Ireland would not again see a battle on the scale of the *Tain* till Brian Boru would rout the Vikings in the eleventh century.

As these transformed warrior children of Patrick's heart lay down the swords of battle, flung away the knives of sacrifice, and cast aside the chains of slavery, they very much remained Irishmen and Irishwomen. Indeed, the survival of an Irish psychological identity is one of the marvels of the Irish story. Unlike the continental church fathers, the Irish never troubled themselves overmuch about eradicating pagan influences, which they tended to wink at and enjoy. The pagan festivals continued to be celebrated, which is why we today can still celebrate the Irish feasts of May Day and Hallowe'en.⸖ To this day, there is a town in Kerry that holds a fertility festival each August, where a magnificent he-goat presides like Cernunnos for three days and nights, and bacchanalian drinking, wild dancing, and varieties of sexual indiscretion are the principal entertainments. It is this characteristically Irish mélange of pagan and Christian that forms the theme of Brian Friel's magnificent play *Dancing at Lughnasa*—Lughnasa being the harvest feast of the god Lug, still celebrated on August 1 in parts of Donegal. Irish marriage customs remained most un-Roman. As late as the twelfth century—seven centuries after the conversion of the Irish to the Gospel—a husband or wife could call it quits and walk out for good on February 1, the feast of Imbolc, which meant that Irish marriages were renewable yearly, like magazine subscriptions or insurance policies. As late as the last century naked men (and, for all we know, women) raced horses bareback along Clare's beaches through the surf at high tide, looking for all the world like their prehistoric warrior ancestors. But after Patrick the eviler gods shrank in stature and became much less troublesome, became in fact the comical gargoyles of medieval imagination, peering fearfully from undignified nooks, and the belief grew strong that the one thing the devil cannot bear is laughter.

Edmund Campion, the Elizabethan Jesuit who was martyred at Ty-

⸖ The first day of May, called Beltaine, was a spring celebration distinguished by bonfires, maypoles, and sexual license; the last night of October, called Samain, marked the beginning of winter, and was a night on which ghosts and other unfriendly creatures from the Otherworld were allowed to frighten the living.

burn in 1581, has left us a description of the Irish that rings true to this day:

> The people are thus inclined: religious, franke, amorous, irefull, sufferable of paines infinite, very glorious, many sorcerers, excellent horsemen, delighted with warres, great almes-givers, [sur]passing in hospitalitie. . . . They are sharpe-witted, lovers of learning, capable of any studie whereunto they bend themselves, constant in travaile, adventerous, intractable, kinde-hearted, secret in displeasure.

We can still make out in this Elizabethan group portrait not only the Irish of our own day but the lively ghosts of Irishmen long past—Ailil, Medb, Cuchulainn, Derdriu, and, after a fashion, Patrick himself. Whether or not Freud was right when he muttered in exasperation that the Irish were the only people who could not be helped by psychoanalysis, there can be no doubt of one thing: the Irish will never change.

The one element in Campion's description that we might not immediately associate with the characters of the *Tain* is his reference to scholarship—"lovers of learning, capable of any studie whereunto they bend themselves." For it was Patrick's Christian mission that nurtured Irish scholarship into blossom. Patrick, the incomplete Roman, nevertheless understood that, though Christianity was not inextricably wedded to Roman custom, it could not survive without Roman literacy.

THE DYING GAUL

The epitome of the Celtic warrior's bravery, this is a Roman copy of a Greek statue made in the third century B.C. The great curved trumpet was one of the musical instruments that made a fearsome racket as part of every Celtic war party's equipage.

CELTIC GODS

The god at bottom right is devouring
a human. Note the details of a bracelet
on the wrist of the victim, the severed
heads of previous victims, and the erect
phallus of the god, who is patently
enjoying himself. (Bouches-du-Rhône,
c. third century B.C.) The idol above
left is a sheela-na-gig, a motif found
throughout Britain and Ireland,
although very difficult to photograph
well because the surviving examples
are in extremely inaccessible nooks
and have usually been damaged by
weather or censorship. The sheela parts
her vulva both as an invitation to sex
and as a reminder of her fertility. Her
face, although sometimes smiling, is
moronic and brutal, and usually
skeletal. She is, like Kali of India,
death-in-life and life-in-death.
(Kilpeck, England.) The figure above
right was found in Tanderagee,
Armagh. The position of its arms,
although difficult to interpret, is
reminiscent of the traditional posture
of some Indian deities.

CELTIC
SANCTUARY
The skull niches in
the remains of a
prehistoric sanctuary
at Bouches-du-
Rhône are evidence
of the centrality of
human sacrifice in
Celtic religion.

CLONFERT CATHEDRAL
The impassive heads
above the doorway of
eleventh-century Clonfert
Cathedral are a kind of
reprise of the display of
severed heads at Bouches-
du-Rhône and other
prehistoric Celtic
sanctuaries. As cathedrals
go, Clonfert is tiny—even
by Irish standards—and
built in the middle of
nowhere, thus suggesting
that this place was chosen
for its ancient druidic
associations.

GUNDESTRUP CAULDRON
The gigantic cook-god on the inner left panel is dropping the human into a boiling vat.

GUNDESTRUP CAULDRON, INNER PANEL
The "Cernunnos" figure with animals and plants. The torque in the figure's right hand is similar to the torque that the Dying Gaul wears around his neck.

GALLARUS

This Kerry oratory, shaped like an upturned boat, is typical of early Irish Christian architecture. In the wall opposite the door, a window faces east and provides light for a small altar, around which barely a dozen people could congregate. The drystone walls have—without any suggestion of mortar—maintained their delicate proportions for some fourteen centuries. Drystone technique, which depends on choosing just the right stone at the right place to achieve a permanent balance, was the same technique that the monks often used to build their individual cells, shaped like beehives.

OGHAM

Stones like this one were used as grave memorials in prehistoric and early Christian Ireland. The lines down one edge represent a man's name. A single line to the left represents B; two lines to the left, L; a single line to the right, H; a slanted line across the edge, M; and so forth. Hardly a swift form of communication.

NEWGRANGE
A vast tumulus, built in the Boyne Valley in the third millennium B.C., contains numerous mysterious rock carvings, such as this one at the entrance.

SOMERSET BOX
A prehistoric bronze box, both mathematical and playful, found in Galway.

BOOK OF KELLS, "CHI-RHO" PAGE

The intricate interlacings at the beginning of Matthew's Gospel are full of surprises for those who take the time to examine them—such as the scene to the lower left of the Rho in which two mice play tug-of-war over a piece of bread, observed by two cats, each surmounted by a mouse. The great letters are the Greek monogram for Christ: Chi, Rho (i.e., X, P in Greek—the sounds *ch* and *r* in English), followed by I. "Chr(ist)i"—meaning "Of Christ"—is the word with which Matthew's Gospel begins.

ARDAGH
CHALICE
The acme of
Irish Christian
metallurgy,
seventh–eighth
century. Even the
underside of the
base, right, is richly
ornamented.

And so the first Irish Christians also became the first Irish literates.

Ireland is unique in religious history for being the only land into which Christianity was introduced without bloodshed. There are no Irish martyrs (at least not till Elizabeth I began to create them eleven centuries after Patrick). And this lack of martyrdom troubled the Irish, to whom a glorious death by violence presented such an exciting finale. If all Ireland had received Christianity without a fight, the Irish would just have to think up some new form of martyrdom—something even more interesting than the wonderfully grisly stories they had begun to learn in the simple continental collections, called "martyrologies," from which Patrick and his successors taught them to read.

The Irish of the late fifth and early sixth centuries soon found a solution, which they called the Green Martyrdom, opposing it to the conventional Red Martyrdom by blood. The Green Martyrs were those who, leaving behind the comforts and pleasures of ordinary human society, retreated to the woods, or to a mountaintop, or to a lonely island—to one of the green no-man's-lands outside tribal jurisdictions—there to study the scriptures and commune with God. For among the story collections Patrick gave them they found the examples of the anchorites of the Egyptian desert, who, also lacking the purification rite of persecution, had lately devised a new form of holiness by living alone in isolated hermitages, braving all kinds of physical and psychological adversity, and imposing on themselves the most heroic fasts and penances, all for the sake of drawing nearer to God.

There is a charming poem in Irish, attributed to one of

Patrick's converts, Saint Manchan of Offaly, in which we can almost trace the history of this movement of the Green Martyrs. In it, the would-be martyr enumerates his simple needs, the first being a lonely hermitage:

> Grant me sweet Christ the grace to find—
> Son of the living God!—
> A small hut in a lonesome spot
> To make it my abode.

But the saintly recluse does not intend to wall himself off from holy intercourse with his fellow humans. A little out of the way, he will still be available to those who walk the extra mile to find insight, instruction, and baptism. Thus, the second stanza—and request number 2:

> A little pool but very clear
> To stand beside the place
> Where all men's sins are washed away
> By sanctifying grace.

The hermit now turns his attention to his eremitical environment, which results in these further requests:

> A pleasant woodland all about
> To shield it [the hut] from the wind,
> And make a home for singing birds
> Before it and behind.

> A southern aspect for the heat
> A stream along its foot,

A smooth green lawn with rich top soil
Propitious to all fruit.

Having established himself as local guru, the typical hermit was soon joined by like-minded seekers, who wished to build their own huts and sit at the master's feet. Thus, the "hermit" continues with his list of godly requests:

My choice of men to live with me
And pray to God as well;
Quiet men of humble mind—
Their number I shall tell.

Four files of three or three of four
To give the psalter forth;
Six to pray by the south church wall
And six along the north.

Two by two my dozen friends—
To tell the number right—
Praying with me to move the King
Who gives the sun its light.

The Irish, who had always been fascinated by numbers and their magical properties, thought twelve, the biblical number that signifies completeness, to be the right count for a religious community, so imitating the arrangement of Christ and his Twelve Apostles. The humble hermit, who began by asking for so little, is now the abbot of a monastery of men who live in small beehive-shaped huts, surrounding a conventual church. As abbot, father to his flock, standing in the place of Christ himself, the former hermit must of course begin to think of his exalted role and of the proper dignity of his church. Thus, a further request:

A lovely church, a home for God
Bedecked with linen fine,
Where over the white Gospel page
The Gospel candles shine.

Having come this far, the "hermit" perceives the need for a common dwelling, ample enough to house the diverse functions of a large, well-established monastery. But the poet still manages to imagine this edifice as diminutive in this request:

A little house where all may dwell
And body's care be sought,
Where none shows lust or arrogance,
None thinks an evil thought.

In the poet's final items, we almost catch a glimpse of monastic culture in full swing, the bustling, wealthy—and untaxed—center of a new Irish civilization, where solitude and quiet may be relatively rare:

And all I ask for housekeeping
I get and pay no fees,
Leeks from the garden, poultry, game,
Salmon and trout and bees.

My share of clothing and of food
From the King of fairest face,
And I to sit at times alone
And pray in every place.

The change in tone and content from the bloodletting of
the *Tain* to the quiet delights of "The Hermit's Song" is worthy of consideration. Humor is abundant in both literatures, but
the harsh humor of the mythological cycle has been transmuted
into a kind of self-deprecatory, monastic mirth. And even
though the gentle rhythm of self-deprecation cannot entirely
suppress the clang of heroic egotism (for the poet surely thinks
quite highly of himself), the characteristic size of men and their
possessions has decreased: everything about Cuchulainn was
outsized; everything about the hermit is endearingly small.
Whereas the colors of the *Tain* were gleaming metals and in-
constant shadows, the world of the hermit shines with a light
that bathes each object, so that all items stand out distinctly and
substantially in their own rich colors, like miniature pictures in
an early Gospel book. Brightness is the central experience here,
and such concepts as clarity, cleanliness, illumination, and fairness suffuse the poem.

So the wished-for extremes of the Green Martyrdom were
largely—and quickly—abandoned in favor of monasticism, a
movement which, though it could support and even nurture
oddity and eccentricity, subjected such tendencies to a social
contract. Since Ireland had no cities, these monastic establishments grew rapidly into the first population centers, hubs of
unprecedented prosperity, art, and learning.

Ireland was still Ireland, so we should not overemphasize

the new unity of its culture. There was still plenty of tribal warfare: sometimes even monasteries took the field against one another. Tales of solitary ecstatics and madmen remained as abundant as ever, whether of Sweeney, the king who thought he was a bird and lived his life in treetops, or of Kevin of Glendalough, a sixth-century hermit who lived in a hole in the rock wall of a cliff, emerging in winter to stand for hours stark naked in the icy waters of the lough⋆ or in summer to hurl himself—again naked—into a bush of poisonous nettles.

But even Kevin eventually gave in and allowed a monastic community to form around him. They

⋆ A glen in Irish is a valley created by cliffs or rocky hillsides. Glendalough is the Glen of the Two Loughs (or Lakes). Kevin preferred to stand in the Upper Lake because it was more remote—and probably chillier.

couldn't all fit into the hole in the cliff (which may still be seen today, four feet wide, seven feet deep, three feet high), so Kevin agreed reluctantly to move to the level shore, where his disciples built a tiny church and for their master a drystone hut shaped like a beehive, a wonder of intuitive Irish engineering that stands to this day, and for themselves daub and wattle huts that have long since disappeared. Though they lived singly, they gathered together to chant the Psalms at the appointed monastic hours, rising twice each night and trundling along to the chapel in the cold and dark to sing their office. This picture of the monks' devotion is preserved for us because one of them used it as his example to explain some archaic words in an Irish grammar he was copying:

The wind over the Hog's Back moans,
It takes the trees and lays them low,
And shivering monks o'er frozen stones
To the twain hours of nighttime go.

Soon enough, even the level shore of the Upper Lake proved inadequate to Kevin's community, for people began to come from all over Ireland to sit at the feet of the monks and learn all they had to teach. On a plain to the east of the Lower Lake, the monks built what would become in time a kind of university city, to which came thousands of hopeful students first from all over Ireland, then from England, and at last from everywhere in Europe. Never forgetting the prehistoric Irish virtue of heroic hospitality, the monks turned no one away, as is confirmed in this description of a typical university city, given to us by the Venerable Bede, first historian of the newly emergent English[*] people:

> Many of the nobles of the English nation and lesser men also had set out thither, forsaking their native island either for the grace of sacred learning or a more austere life. And some of them indeed soon dedicated themselves faithfully to the monastic life, others rejoiced rather to give themselves to learning, going about from one master's cell to another. All these the Irish willingly received, and saw to it to supply them with food day by day without cost, and books for their studies, and teaching, free of charge.

[*] In Patrick's time the island of Britain was peopled by Romanized Celts, whom we call Britons, and, in its northern reaches, by the un-Romanized and ferocious Picts, who painted pictures all over their bodies, horrifying the Romans, who called them *Picti* (Painted People). Patrick was a Romanized Celtic Briton—*not* an Englishman. The German Angles, who in Patrick's day were—with their Germanic cousins the Saxons and Jutes— harrying the southern and eastern coasts of Britain, soon settled in Britain, pushing the Romanized Celts into Wales and Cornwall. These new people, pagan at first but evangelized in the seventh century by a Roman librarian named Augustine *(not* of Hippo), gave their name to their new home, which came to be called Angland, or England.

From the careful Bede we learn, therefore, that the Irish monastic universities accepted commoners as well as noblemen and those who wished for learning but not the cloister.

Irish generosity extended not only to a variety of people but to a variety of ideas. As unconcerned about orthodoxy of thought as they were about uniformity of monastic practice, they brought into their libraries everything they could lay their hands on. They were resolved to shut out nothing. Not for them the scruples of Saint Jerome, who feared he might burn in hell for reading Cicero. Once they had learned to read the Gospels and the other books of the Holy Bible, the lives of the martyrs and ascetics, and the sermons and commentaries of the fathers of the church, they began to devour all of the old Greek and Latin pagan literature that came their way. In their unrestrained catholicity, they shocked conventional churchmen, who had been trained to value Christian literature principally and give a wide berth to the dubious morality of the pagan classics. A learned British ecclesiastic, Aldhelm of Malmesbury, who had himself been educated by the Irish (and so knew whereof he spoke), wrote to warn a young Saxon student against the "ancient fables" and other temptations of an Irish education: "What advantage does it bring to the sacrament of the orthodox faith to sweat over reading and studying the polluted lewdness of Proserpine, or Hermione, the wanton offspring of Menelaus and Helen, or the Lupercalia and the votaries of Priapus?" Aldhelm—you can almost hear the sniffy intake of breath—had learned his lessons well and could still, apparently, break out in a sweat when one of the racier classical tales danced through his monkish head.

It was not that the Irish were uncritical, just that they saw no value in self-imposed censorship. They could have said with Terence, *"Homo sum: humani nil a me alienum puto"* ("I am a human being, so nothing human is strange to me"). To John T. McNeill, that most balanced of all church historians, it was precisely "the breadth and richness of Irish monastic learning, derived from the classical . . . authors" that was about to give Ireland its "unique role in the history of Western culture."

Though the timeworn tales of Greece and Rome were fresh and fascinating to them, the Irish monks could occasionally take a dimmer view of their own literature, which we have only because they copied it down, either from childhood memories or from the performance of wandering bards. In the Book of Leinster, which contains a florid version of the *Tain,* the epic ends with a monastic "Amen," after which the scribe wrote down in Irish the earlier oral culture's bardic formula: "A blessing on everyone who will memorize the Tain faithfully in this form, and not put any other form on it." Just after this in Latin the same scribe left this succinct critique: "I who have copied down this story, or more accurately fantasy, do not credit the details of the story, or fantasy. Some things in it are devilish lies, and some are poetical figments; some seem possible and others not; some are for the enjoyment of idiots."

So, though he disapproved of its contents, he copied out the *Tain.* It is thanks to such scribes, however cranky their glosses may sometimes be, that we have the rich trove of early Irish literature, the earliest vernacular literature of Europe to survive—because it was taken seriously enough to be written down. Though these early Irish literates were intensely interested in the worlds opened up to them by the three sacred languages of Greek, Latin, and—in a rudimentary form—Hebrew, they loved their own tongue too much ever to stop using it. Whereas elsewhere in Europe, no educated man would be caught dead speaking a vernacular, the Irish thought that all language was a game—and too much fun to be deprived of any part of it. They were still too childlike and playful to find any value in snobbery.

Here and there in the surviving manuscripts—at the tail end of a convoluted Latin translation of a Pauline letter, in the margins of an impenetrable Greek commentary on scripture— we find the bored scribblings of the Irish scribes, who kept themselves awake by writing out a verse or two of a beloved

Irish lyric—and so, by accumulation, left for our enjoyment a whole literature that would otherwise be unknown. Sometimes the scribe may be composing his own lyric, for all we know; and often enough he is likely to have been a student—not always, given the character of his daydreams, a boy headed for a monastic vocation. "The son of the King of Moy," writes one scribbler,

> Found a girl in the greenwood in Midsummer.
> She gave him lapfuls of blackberries.
> She gave him armfuls of strawberries.

Another is even more direct:

> He is a heart,
> An acorn from the oakwood:
> He is young.
> Kiss him!

And a third is in real danger of failing to complete his studies:

> All are keen
> To know who'll sleep with blond Aideen.
> All Aideen herself will own
> Is that she will not sleep alone.

One scribe will complain of the backbreaking work of book-copying, another of a sloppy fellow scribe: "It is easy to spot Gabrial's work here" is written in a beautiful hand at the margin of an undistinguished page. A third will grind his teeth about the difficulty of the tortured ancient Greek that he is copying: "There's an end to that—and seven curses with it!"

But for the most part they enjoy their work and find themselves engrossed in the stories they are copying. Beneath a description of the death of Hector on the Plain of Troy, one scribe, completely absorbed in the words he is copying, has written most sincerely: "I am greatly grieved at the above-mentioned death." Another, measuring the endurance of his beloved art against his own brief life span, concludes: "Sad it is, little parti-colored white book, for a day will surely come when someone will say over your page: 'The hand that wrote this is no more.' "

Perhaps the clearest picture we possess of what it was like to be a scribal scholar is contained in a four-stanza Irish poem slipped into a ninth-century manuscript, which otherwise contains such learned material as a Latin commentary on Virgil and a list of Greek paradigms:

I and Pangur Ban my cat,
'Tis a like task we are at:
Hunting mice is his delight,
Hunting words I sit all night.

'Tis a merry thing to see
At our tasks how glad are we,
When at home we sit and find
Entertainment to our mind.

'Gainst the wall he sets his eye,
Full and fierce and sharp and sly;

'Gainst the wall of knowledge I
All my little wisdom try.

So in peace our task we ply,
Pangur Ban my cat and I;
In our arts we find our bliss,
I have mine and he has his.

These were happy human beings, occasionally waspish, but normally filled with delight at the tasks their fate had set for them. They did not see themselves as drones. Rather, they engaged the text they were working on, tried to comprehend it after their fashion, and, if possible, add to it, even improve on it. In this dazzling new culture, a book was not an isolated document on a dusty shelf; book truly spoke to book, and writer to scribe, and scribe to reader, from one generation to the next. These books were, as we would say in today's jargon, open, interfacing, and intertextual—glorious literary smorgasbords in which the scribe often tried to include a bit of everything, from every era, language, and style known to him. No one would see their like again till James Joyce would write *Ulysses*.

At the center of this new Irish universe, the "Gospel candles shine" on the "white Gospel page," as in "The Hermit's Song." Like the Jews before them, the Irish enshrined literacy as their central religious act. In a land where literacy had previously been unknown, in a world where the old literate civilizations were sinking fast beneath successive waves of barbarism, the white Gospel page, shining in all the little oratories of Ireland, acted as a pledge: the lonely darkness had been turned into light, and the lonely virtue of courage, sustained through all the centuries, had been transformed into hope.

The Irish received literacy in their own way, as something to play with. The only alphabet they'd ever known was prehistoric Ogham, a cumbersome set of lines based on the Roman alphabet, which they incised laboriously into the corners of standing stones to turn them into memorials. These rune-like inscriptions, which continued to appear in the early years of the Christian period, hardly suggested what would happen next, for within a generation the Irish had mastered Latin and even Greek and, as best they could, were picking up some Hebrew. As we have seen already, they devised Irish grammars, and copied out the whole of their native oral literature. All this was fairly straightforward, too straightforward once they'd got the hang of it. They began to make up languages. The members of a far-flung secret society, formed as early as the late fifth century (barely a generation after the Irish had become literate), could write to one another in impenetrably erudite, never-before-spoken patterns of Latin, called *Hisperica Famina,* not unlike the dream-language of *Finnegans Wake* or even the languages J. R. R. Tolkien would one day make up for his hobbits and elves.

Nothing brought out Irish playfulness more than the copying of the books themselves, a task no reader of the ancient world could entirely neglect. At the outset there were in Ireland no scriptoria to speak of, just individual hermits and monks, each in his little beehive cell or sitting outside in fine weather, copying a needed text from a borrowed book, old book on one knee, fresh sheepskin pages on the other. Even at their grandest, these were simple, out-of-doors people. (As late as the ninth century an Irish annotator describes himself as writing under a greenwood tree while listening to a clear-voiced cuckoo hopping from bush to bush.) But they found the shapes of letters magical. Why, they asked themselves, did a *B* look the way it did? Could it look some other way? Was there an essential *B*-ness? The result of such why-is-the-sky-blue questions was a new kind of book, the Irish codex; and one after another, Ireland began to produce the most spectacular, magical books the world had ever seen.

From its earliest manifestations literacy had a decorative aspect. How could it be otherwise, since implicit in all pictograms, hieroglyphs, and letters is some cultural esthetic, some answer to the question, What is most beautiful? The Mesoamerican answer lies in looped and bulbous rock carvings, the Chinese answer in vibrantly minimalist brush strokes, the ancient Egyptian answer in stately picture puzzles. Even alphabets, those most abstract and frozen forms of communication, embody an esthetic, which changes depending on the culture of its user. How unlike one another the carved, unyielding Roman alphabet of Augustus's triumphal arches and the idiosyncratically homely Romano-Germanic alphabet of Gutenberg's Bible.

For their part, the Irish combined the stately letters of the Greek and Roman alphabets with the talismanic, spellbinding simplicity of Ogham to produce initial capitals and headings that rivet one's eyes to the page and hold the reader in awe. As late as the twelfth century, Geraldus Cambrensis was forced to conclude that the Book of Kells was "the work of an angel, not of a man." Even today, Nicolete Gray in *A History of Lettering* can say of its great "Chi-Rho" page that the three Greek characters—the monogram of Christ—are "more presences than letters."

For the body of the text, the Irish developed two hands, one a dignified but rounded script called Irish half-uncial, the other an easy-to-write script called Irish minuscule that was more readable, more fluid, and, well, happier than anything devised by the Romans. Recommended by its ease and readability, this second hand would be adopted by a great many scribes far beyond the borders of Ireland, becoming the common script of the Middle Ages.

*Irish majuscule or half-uncial, Book of Durrow,
seventh century*

*Irish minuscule in the Saint Gall manuscript of
Priscian's Grammar (c. 850)*

As decoration for the texts of their most precious books, the Irish instinctively found their models not in the crude lines of Ogham, but in their own prehistoric mathematics and their own most ancient evidence of the human spirit—the megalithic tombs of the Boyne Valley. These tombs had been constructed in Ireland about 3000 B.C. in the same eon that Stonehenge was built in Britain. Just as mysterious as Stonehenge, both for their provenance and the complexity of their engineering, these great barrow graves are

Ireland's earliest architecture and are faced by the indecipher-
able spirals, zigzags, and lozenges of Ireland's earliest art.
These massive tumuli, telling a story we can now only specu-
late on,[*] had long provided Irish smiths with their artistic inspiration. For in the sweeping lines of the Boyne's intriguing
carvings, we can discern the ultimate sources of the magnificent metal jewelry and other objects that were being made at
the outset of the Patrician period by smiths who, in Irish society, had the status of seers.

Brooches, boxes, discs, scabbards, clips, and horse trappings
of the time all proclaim their devotion to the models of the
Boyne Valley carvings. But this intricate riot of metalwork,
allowing for subtleties impossible in stone, is like a series of riffs
on the original theme. What was that theme? Balance in im-
balance. Take, for instance, the witty cover on the bronze box
that is part of the Somerset Hoard from Galway: precisely
mathematical yet deliberately (one might almost say perversely)
off-center, forged by a smith of expert compass and twinkling
eye. It is endlessly fascinating because, as a riff on circularity, it
has no end. It seems to say, with the spirals of Newgrange,
"There is no circle; there is only the spiral, the endlessly recon-
figurable spiral. There are no straight lines, only curved ones."
Or, to recall the most characteristic of all Irish responses when
faced with the demand for a plain, unequivocal answer: "Well,
it is, and it isn't." "She does, and
she doesn't." "You will, and you
won't."

This sense of balance in imbal-
ance, of riotous complexity moving
swiftly within a basic unity, would
now find its most extravagant ex-

[*] A surprisingly coherent theory, found in Martin Brennan, *The Boyne Valley Vision* (Portlaoise, 1980), is that the carvings on the Boyne tombs constitute an ancient sky map and calendar, predictive, like Stonehenge, of celestial events.

pression in Irish Christian art—in the monumental high crosses, in miraculous liturgical vessels such as the Ardagh Chalice, and, most delicately of all, in the art of the Irish codex.

Codex was used orginally to distinguish a book, as we know it today, from its ancestor, the scroll. By Patrick's time the codex had almost universally displaced the scroll, because a codex was so much easier to dip into and peruse than a cumbersome scroll, which had the distinct disadvantage of snapping back into a roll the moment one became too absorbed in the text. The pages of most books were of mottled parchment, that is, dried sheepskin, which was universally available—and nowhere more abundant than in Ireland, whose bright green fields still host each April an explosion of new white lambs. Vellum, or calfskin, which was more uniformly white when dried, was used more sparingly for the most honored texts. (The "white Gospel page" of "The Hermit's Song" is undoubtedly vellum.) It is interesting to consider that the shape of the modern book, taller than wide, was determined by the dimensions of a sheepskin, which could most economically be cut into double pages that yield our modern book shape when folded. The scribe transcribed the text onto pages gathered into a booklet called a quire, later stitched with other quires into a larger volume, which was then sometimes bound between protecting covers. Books and pamphlets of less consequence were often left unbound. Thus, a form of the "cheap paperback" was known even in the fifth century.

The most famous Irish codex is the Book of Kells, kept in the library of Trinity College, Dublin, but dozens of others survive, their names—the Book of Echternach, for instance, or the Book of Maihingen—sometimes giving us an idea of how far they traveled from the Irish scriptoria that were their primeval source. Astonishingly decorated Irish manuscripts of the early medieval period are today the great jewels of libraries in England, France, Switzerland, Germany, Sweden, Italy, and even Russia. How did they get there? The answer lies with the greatest Irish figure after Patrick, Columcille, prince of Clan Conaill, born in the royal enclosure of Gartan, on December 7, 521, less than ninety years after Patrick's arrival as bishop.

Though he could have been a king, maybe even high king, Columcille chose to become a monk. His real name, Crimthann, or Fox, holds an echo of the ancient mythology, and he was probably red-haired. The name Columcille, or Dove of the Church, was his later monastic nickname. This may be ironic, as we shall soon see (and it was, in any case, Romanized as Columba, the name under which he usually appears in accounts written outside Ireland). Educated in the bardic traditions of his ancestors and then—under Bishop Finian of Clonard—in the new tradition of Christian learning, he journeyed as far as Gaul to visit the tomb of Saint Martin of Tours, whose sensible monastic rule was finding favor on the continent not only with bishops who feared the movement of single-minded, wild-eyed anchorites, but with men who wished to escape the increasing uncertainties of an age of upheaval. Returning to Ireland, the energetic Columcille began founding monasteries with a will—at Durrow, Kells, and many other places—so that, by the time he reached the age of forty-one, forty-one Irish foundations could claim him as their royal patron.

An intense man, Columcille loved beautiful things, the heritage no doubt of his privileged childhood, and was especially sensitive to the *genius loci* of Derry—"angel-haunted Derry," he called it—where he founded his first monastery (even before his pilgrimage to Tours) and of which he sang in sensuous poetry that can stand beside any in the early Irish canon. But if Columcille loved anything more than his native place, he loved books, especially beautifully designed manuscripts. As a student, he had fallen in love with his master's psalter, a uniquely decorated book of great price. He resolved to make his own copy by stealth, and so we find him sitting in Finian's church at Moville, hunched over the coveted psalter, copying it in the dark. According to legend, he had no candle, but the five fingers of his left hand shone like so many lights while his right hand assiduously copied. The legend is embellished with many such details; but the sum and substance of it is that Columcille was found out and brought before King Diarmait, who issued his famous decision: "To every cow her calf; to every book its copy." It was history's first copyright case.

Columcille, forced to return the copy to Finian, was too much the aristocratic pagan to forget his humiliation. (Remember, it was his own Clan Conaill that continued to mate a new king with a mare.) When, sometime later, one of Columcille's followers was killed on Diarmait's orders, the princely monk seized his opportunity. God, he claimed, who protected all monks, had to be avenged. Mobilizing his powerful kinsmen, he took the field against Diarmait's forces and beat them decisively. When the clash of battle had subsided, three thousand and one lay dead, only one of them on princely Columcille's side. The contested psalter, which, needless to say, came to Columcille among the spoils of victory, was ever after called the Cathach, or Warrior.

But Columcille's victory had less pleasant consequences for

him. For a time he was excommunicated, the customary punishment for a monk who takes up arms, and his penance was permanent exile from his beloved Ireland: he must now reach heaven by a voyage of no return, and in his exile he must save as many souls as perished in the battle he precipitated. Columcille set out with twelve doughty companions, sailing north beyond the horizon and finally reaching the island of Iona, off the west coast of the land we call Scotland—just far enough north so that (as Columcille insisted) there is never a view of Ireland. As Columcille makes his journey, which would forever change the course of western history, let us pause for a moment to reflect on the world he leaves behind and the world that he and his disciples are sailing toward.

The Green Martyrdom had been a failure, both because of the apparently unquenchable Irish tendency to sociability and, perhaps even more important, because of the natural fertility of Ireland itself, which possessed nothing resembling an Egyptian desert and almost no place that did not, with a little foresight, abound in "leeks from the garden, poultry, game, salmon and trout and bees." In the early days, soon after the time of Patrick, the anarchistic anchorites sought out rocky islands for their hermitages, places like Inis Murray and Skellig Michael off the western coast. "It is hard to believe," wrote Kenneth Clark, "that for quite a long time—almost a hundred years—western Christianity survived by clinging to places like Skellig Michael, a pinnacle of rock eighteen miles from the Irish coast, rising seven hundred feet out of the sea." (The hundred years of which he speaks stretch from the late fifth century, after Patrick's death, to the late sixth century, by which time, as we shall see, the Irish monks had reconnected barbarized Europe to the traditions of Christian literacy.) But the anchorites survived only too well, even in this rocky terrain, by dining on seabirds and cultivating small, rich gardens, fertilized by seaweed. They added to their numbers, built their beehive huts, copied their books, and thrived—as did, at least in these far-flung Irish places, western Christianity.

Soon enough, cityless Ireland altered, without quite meaning to, the political structure of Christianity, which had been based on bishoprics that had mimicked Roman urban administrative units, called dioceses. Lacking cities, Ireland didn't quite see the point of bishops, and gradually these were replaced in importance by abbots and—in a development that would make any self-respecting Roman's blood run cold—abbesses. Though our sources are imperfect and incomplete, there is little doubt that bishops turned into something like chaplans to various royal families, whose own power in the new Christian dispensation was somewhat on the wane, while abbots and abbesses came to rule over increasingly large and powerful monastic communities. The power of the druids, who had lived and worshiped in sacred groves, had been easily handed over to the Green Martyrs, who also lived and worshiped in sacred groves. But the access of the new, literate druids (the monastic successors of the Green Martyrs) to the books of the Greco-Roman library—that is, to the whole of the classical sciences and the wisdom of the ancients—gradually created new centers of knowledge and wealth such as Ireland had never known.

In these new monastic city-states, a woman could reign as Medb had once done over Connacht. Brigid of Kildare, a convert of Patrick's (and, perhaps, the noblewoman he describes as *"pulcherrima"*), ruled as high abbess of an immense double monastery—that is, a foundation that admitted both men and women, another irregularity that would have deeply offended

Roman Catholic sensibility, which to this day imagines rule by a woman over men as a perversion of the natural order. Brigid's druidical associations would also have been troubling to such a sensibility. She is reputed to have taken the veil on the Hill of Uisnech, Ireland's primeval navel and the mythical center of its cosmic mandala. Her monastery began as a sort of Green Martyrdom under a huge oak, the sacred tree of the druids—thus, Kildare, which means "Church of the Oak."

As with Columcille, much of the material surrounding Brigid is too suffused with miraculous happenings to be mistaken for history (she is said, for instance, to have been able to hang her cloak from a sunbeam), but a personality comes through as palpable as Medb's. She even delivers her lines with Maevian pithiness. When, for example, her charioteer, attempting a shortcut, overturns their vehicle, poker-faced Brigid rises from the wreck, dusts herself off, and remarks only: "Shortcuts make broken bones."

Following her conversion, her father, an extremely wealthy man, was appalled to find his beautiful daughter giving away his stores to beggars. Quite out of control, he threw Brigid into the back of his chariot, screaming: "It is neither out of kindness nor honor that I take you for a ride: I am going to sell you to the King of Leinster to grind his corn." Arriving at the king's enclosure, the father "unbuckled his sword, leaving it in the chariot beside Brigid, so that—out of respect—he could approach the king unarmed." No sooner had the father gone off than a leper appeared, begging Brigid for her help. Since the only thing handy was her father's sword, she gave it to him. Meanwhile, the father was making his offer to the king, who must have smelled something fishy, and insisted on meeting the girl before accepting. When king and father came out to the chariot, the father noticed immediately that his sword was missing and demanded to know where it was. When Brigid told him, "he flew into a wild rage" and began to beat her.

"Stop," cried the king, and called Brigid to him. "Why do you steal your father's property and give it away?"

"If I had the power," answered Brigid, "I would steal all your royal wealth, and give it to Christ's brothers and sisters." The king quickly declined the father's kind offer because "your daughter is too good for me."

It is not surprising that, after she escaped from her father and became abbess, Brigid's monastery was famous for its hospitality. This is the table grace associated with her name:

I should like a great lake of finest ale
For the King of kings.
I should like a table of the choicest food
For the family of heaven.
Let the ale be made from the fruits of faith,
And the food be forgiving love.

I should welcome the poor to my feast,
For they are God's children.
I should welcome the sick to my feast,
For they are God's joy.
Let the poor sit with Jesus at the highest place,
And the sick dance with the angels.

God bless the poor,
God bless the sick,
And bless our human race.
God bless our food,

God bless our drink,
All homes, O God, embrace.

However unorthodox Brigid's rule by Roman standards, it is easy to see from the tales about her how Christian faith, which was strong enough to deprive a tyrant of his sword, unman a king, and empower the powerless, impressed this warrior society. It would be reckless overstatement to claim that women possessed equality in Irish society; but their larger presence here ensured a greater stress on physical amenities ("a clean house, a big fire, and a couch without sorrow" were among the many requisites of monastic hospitality) and on the value of intimacy (Ita, a sixth-century hermit-foundress was thought to have been granted the ecstatic privilege of nursing the Christ Child at her own virgin breasts). This larger female presence also contributed to the teeming variety of Irish religious life—a variety that would have distressed the Romans, had they known of it. They would have been even more disturbed had they known of the wide-ranging activities of the high abbesses, whose hands had the power to heal, who almost certainly heard confessions, probably ordained clergy, and may even have celebrated Mass.

Such goings-on, though of great antiquity, still have the power to shock the more piously orthodox. *The Old Life of Brigid* claims that Brigid was consecrated bishop "by mistake." Another biography, written in the seventh century by the somewhat simpering Cogitosus, who seems to be trying to curry favor with his superior, omits this information, but one can read between the lines that Cogitosus knew the old story and chose to omit it, for he shows us Brigid preaching—an apostolic or priestly act—and Brigid "on God's business" making "her pontifical way." In his introduction, he effectively admits her to have been bishop in all but name. We know for certain that Brigid and her successor abbesses had a coadjutor bishop who reported to them; and we also know that at this period deacons, not just priests and bishops, offered Mass in parts of Gaul. So a woman bishop may not have appeared as singular as she would today.

Respect for differences was written into the rule books of the Irish monasteries. "Different is the condition of everyone," cautions the Rule of Saint Carthage, "and different the nature of each place." Irish abbots suggested; they did not enforce. And though the abbacy often passed from father to son, another irregularity that would have alarmed the Romans, the Irish balanced their aristocratic preoccupation with lineage by a refreshingly democratic principle: "A man is better than his descent," insists a law of this period, thus asserting the primacy of individual spirit over common blood. Perhaps nothing would have distressed the Romans as much as the way these monks shrugged off the great Roman virtue of Order. In an instruction to his brothers, Columbanus, whom we shall soon meet, affirmed the great Gospel virtue over all else: *"Amor non tenet ordinem"* ("Love has nothing to do with order").

The Irish also developed a form of confession that was exclusively private and that had no equivalent on the continent. In the ancient church, confession of one's sins—and the subsequent penance (such as appearing for years by the church door in sackcloth and ashes)—had always been public. Sin was thought to be a public matter, a crime against the church, which was the Mystical Body of Christ. Some sins were even considered unforgivable, and the forgivable ones could be forgiven only once. Penance was a once-in-a-lifetime sacrament: a second theft, a second adultery and you were "outside the church," irreversibly excommunicated, headed for damnation. By Patrick's day, a kind of private confession was not entirely unknown, but it was still linked to some form of public revelation (remember Patrick's pain in this regard) and liturgical penance. The Irish innovation was to make all confession a completely private affair between penitent and priest—and to make it as repeatable as necessary. (In fact, repetition was encouraged on the theory that, oh well, *everyone* pretty much sinned just about *all* the time.) This adaptation did away with public humiliation out of tenderness for the sinner's feelings, and softened the unyielding penances of the patristic period so that the sinner would not lose heart. But it also emphasized the Irish sense that personal conscience took precedence over public opinion or church authority. The penitent was not labeled by others; he labeled himself. His sin was no one's business but God's.

Though one's confession was made to a human being, he or she was chosen by the penitent for qualities of true priestliness —holiness, wisdom, generosity, loyalty, and courage. No one could ever pry knowledge gained in confession from such a priest, who knew that every confession was sealed forever by God himself. To break that seal was to imperil one's salvation: it was practically the only sin the Irish considered unforgivable. So one did not necessarily choose one's "priest" from among ordained professionals: the act of confession was too personal and too important for such a limitation. One looked for an *anmchara,* a soul-friend, someone to be trusted over a whole lifetime. Thus, the oft-found saying "Anyone without a soul-friend is like a body without a head," which dates from pagan times. The druids, not the monks, had been the first soul-friends.

It is a shame that private confession is one of the few Irish innovations that passed into the universal church. How different might Catholicism be today if it had taken over the easy Irish sympathy between churchmen and laymen and the easy Irish attitudes toward diversity, authority, the role of women, and the relative unimportance of sexual mores. In one of Cogitosus's best stories, tenderhearted Brigid makes the fetus of a nun (whose womb had, "through youthful desire of pleasure, . . . swelled with child") magically disappear ("without coming to birth, and without pain"), so that the nun won't be turned out of her convent. Lucky nun, "returned . . . to health" and no longer pregnant. The story is reminiscent of one told in later times on the continent about a restless young nun who, having escaped her convent, lives a riotous life in the world and returns at the end of her days expecting the worst, only to find that the Virgin Mary has kindly taken her place during her long absence—and no one is the wiser. But it's a bit of a stretch to imagine Cogitosus receiving an episcopal imprimatur for the disappearing fetus nowadays.

Cogitosus is on firmer historical ground when he describes Brigid's foundation of Kildare as it appeared in the mid-seventh century when he himself was a monk there and the church, built after her death to accommodate the masses of pilgrims, was the largest structure in Ireland:

> But who could convey in words the supreme beauty of her church and the countless wonders of her city, of which we would speak? "City" is the right word for it: that so many people are living there justifies the title. It is a great metropolis, within whose outskirts—which Saint Brigid marked out with a clearly defined boundary—no

earthly adversary is feared, nor any incursion of enemies. For the city is the safest place of refuge among all the towns of the whole land of the Irish, with all their fugitives. It is a place where the treasures of kings are looked after, and it is reckoned to be supreme in good order.

And who could number the varied crowds and countless people who gather in from all territories? Some come for the abundance of festivals; others come to watch the crowds go by; others come with great gifts to the celebration of the birth into heaven of Saint Brigid who, on the First of February, falling asleep, safely laid down the burden of her flesh and followed the Lamb of God into the heavenly mansions.

February 1 is also Imbolc, a feast dedicated to the Irish fertility goddess, also named Brigid.

Why were the Romans unaware of these Irish developments? Were the Irish heretics without standing? The year of Columcille's departure for Iona was 564, roughly a century after the death of Patrick, and the truth is that there were few Romans left in western Europe. The vast hordes of Vandals, Sueves, and Alans who had broken through Roman ranks and crossed the frozen Rhine in the first decade of the fifth century had spread throughout Gaul, pillaging and destroying as they went, stopping only when they reached the barrier of the Pyrenees. From there they poured east and west into the neighboring provinces; and this invasion was to be followed by many others. By the early sixth century, successive waves of German barbarians had altered the map of western Europe irrevocably. By mid-century, Salvian is writing that Trier, the center of Roman military government, has been four times laid waste, that Cologne is "overflowing with the enemy," that Mainz is rubble. Not only are the Roman provinces gone, the whole subtle substructure of Roman political organization and Roman communication has vanished. In its place have grown the sturdy little principalities of the Middle Ages, Gothic illiterates ruling over Gothic illiterates, pagan or occasionally Arian—that is, following a debased, simpleminded form of Christianity in which Jesus was given a status similar to that of Mohammed in Islam.

The Irish did not especially mean to be deviant, but their world hardly abounded in models of Christian orthodoxy. After Patrick, they experienced an influx of anchorites and monks fleeing before the barbarian hordes, and these no doubt provided them with some finer points on eremitical and conventual life. "All the learned men on this side of the sea," claims a note in a Leyden manuscript of this time, "took flight for transmarine places like Ireland, bringing about a great increase of learning"—and, doubtlessly, a spectacular increase in the number of books—"to the inhabitants of those regions." But not a few of these men were bone-thin ascetics from such Roman hinterlands as Armenia, Syria, and the Egyptian desert. The Ulster monastery of Bangor, for instance, claimed in its litany to be *"ex Aegypto transducta"* ("translated from Egypt"); and the convention of using red dots to adorn manuscript initials, a convention that soon became a mark of Irish manuscripts, had first been glimpsed by the Irish in books that the fleeing Copts brought with them. The steely zealotry and peculiar practices of such men had already merited the suspicion of orthodox bishops on the continent, who much preferred the rule of Saint Martin of Gaul, whose foundations were all alike and readily subservient to the desires of the local bishop. Soon they would find even greater virtue in the rule of Benedict of Nursia, whose foundation at Monte Cassino would become in time the motherhouse of western monasticism, a monasticism of disciplined uniformity, enforced—through floggings, if necessary—by an autocratic abbot. Blessed by successive popes, the Rule of Saint Benedict would in the end obliterate all memory of the pluriform Irish.

To the Irish, the pope, the bishop of Rome who was successor to Saint Peter, was a kind of high king of the church, but like the high king a distant figure whose wishes were little known and less considered. Rome was surely the ultimate pilgrim's destination—especially because there were books there that could be brought back and copied! But if your motive was holiness:

> To go to Rome
> Is little profit, endless pain;
> The Master that you seek in Rome,
> You find at home, or seek in vain.

The western empire was scarcely a memory now. The last Latin emperor had fallen just a few years after Patrick died. And though there was still a Greek emperor in the east at Constantinople, where a small, defensible state was long established on the Bosporus, he might as well have been at Timbuktu for all his law was known in western lands. All the great continental libraries had vanished; even memory of them had been erased from the minds of those who lived in the emerging feudal societies of medieval Europe. The first three public libraries had been established at Rome under the reign of Augustus, and by the time of Constantine there were twenty-eight. By the end of

Western Europe in the early sixth century

the fourth century, if we are to believe one writer, Ammianus Marcellinus, who may be indulging in hyperbole, *"Bibliotecis sepulcrorum ritu in perpetuum clausis"* ("The libraries, like tombs, were closed forever"). By the end of the fifth century, at any rate, the profession of copyist had pretty much disappeared, and what books were copied were copied personally by the last literate nobles for their own dwindling libraries. In the sixth century, Pope Gregory established a kind of library at Rome. Gregory, the most towering continental figure of his time and rightly called "the Great," took as dim a view of the pagan classics as Aldhelm, and could read no Greek. His library was a poor one. Even so, the resentful, illiterate mob tried to destroy its few books during a famine, for by now the Catholic bishops had become like islands in a barbarian sea. In Italy and Gaul, some book trading continued—much of it with wandering Irish monks—and by century's end Isidore was building a real library in Seville, which consisted of about fifteen presses (or book cabinets), containing perhaps some four hundred bound codices, an amazing number for the time. The only other continental library known to us in this period was in Calabria at Cassiodorus's monkish estate, which he called Vivarium, but the fate of this library is lost in the blood and smoke of the sixth century. Gregory of Tours wrote this sad epitaph on sixth-century literacy: "In these times when the practice of letters declines, no, rather perishes in the cities of Gaul, there has been found no scholar trained in ordered composition to present in prose or verse a picture of the things which have befallen."

Ireland, at peace and furiously copying, thus stood in the position of becoming Europe's publisher. But the pagan Saxon settlements of southern England had cut Ireland off from easy commerce with the continent. While Rome and its ancient empire faded from memory and a new, illiterate Europe rose on its ruins, a vibrant, literary culture was blooming in secret along its Celtic fringe. It needed only one step more to close the circle, which would reconnect Europe to its own past by way of scribal Ireland.

Columcille provided that step. By stepping into the coracle that bore him beyond the horizon, he entered the Irish pantheon of heroes who had done immortal deeds against impossible odds. As he sailed off that morning, he was doing the hardest thing an Irishman could do, a much harder thing than giving up his life: he was leaving Ireland. If the Green Martyrdom had failed, here was a martyrdom that was surely the equal of the Red; and henceforth, all who followed Columcille's lead were called to the White Martyrdom, they who sailed into the white sky of morning, into the unknown, never to return.

In this way, the Irish monastic tradition began to spread beyond Ireland. Already, the Irish monasteries had hosted many thousands of foreign students, who were bringing back Irish learning to their places of origin. Now, Irish monks would themselves colonize barbarized Europe, bringing their learning with them. Scotland, their first outpost, was peopled by indigenous Picts and Irish colonists who had already established themselves in Patrick's time.✦ Never interested in impressive edifices, Irish monks preferred to spend their time in study, prayer, farming—and, of course, copying. So the basic plan of the Iona monastery was quickly executed: a little hut for each monk; an abbot's hut, somewhat larger and on higher ground; a refectory and kitchen; a scriptorium and library; a smithy, a kiln, a mill, and a couple of barns; a modest church—and they were in business. Soon they found they needed one more building, the surprising addition of a guesthouse, for the never-ending stream of visitors had begun—Scots, Picts, Irish, Britons, even Anglo-Saxons—attracted by the reputation of the larger-than-life abbot of Iona. They began to pour into this remote island, and many of them never went home again.

Thus, the indefatigable Columcille began to dream of opening new monasteries. Among the rugged Scots and the scary Picts, especially, Columcille's reputation spread like wildfire. (There wasn't, after all, much going on up that way.) He made one hundred fifty monks the cutoff number for the

✦ In late antiquity and through the Middle Ages, the Irish were called *Scotti* or *Scoti* in Latin, and *Scotus* at the end of a name denoted Irish ancestry. Ireland was called *Hibernia,* sometimes *Scotia* in Latin. *Scotia Minor,* the name applied to the Irish colony in northern Britain, was eventually shortened to *Scotia,* or Scotland.

Iona community, and after they had exceeded that, twelve and one monks would set off to establish another foundation in a new setting. Fresh applicants kept arriving in droves. By the time of Columcille's death in the last days of the sixth century, sixty monastic communities had been founded in his name along the jagged inlets and mountainy heights of windswept Scotland. He had long since passed his quota of three thousand and one souls saved.

No mention of Patrick is made in Columcille's *Life,* which is not so surprising when you consider that it was written by Adomnan, abbot of Iona a hundred years after Columcille's time, when Iona, Kildare, and other early Christian establishments were hotly contending with Patrick's Armagh for the primacy of Christian Ireland. But the personality of Columcille, which gleams through all his works and all the tales we know of him, convinces us that he is Patrick's spiritual son and worthy successor. He is full of fellow feeling, healing the sick by his touch, casting "down into hell" the despoilers of his friend's house, even stopping to restore a wife's lost affection for her husband through protracted conversation and prayer. He is hard on himself, sleeping each night, like Jacob, with a rock for his pillow. He lives in easy communion with nature, speaking to forest animals and nicely managing our first recorded encounter with the Loch Ness Monster (who takes one look at Columcille's upraised arm and makes a quick exit for the lake).

On one occasion, he even returned to Ireland (never say never of an Irish saint) to plead before the national convention meeting in Drumceatt that the Irish kingdom of Dalriada (which covered Irish Scotland and part of Ulster—and to which Columcille owed allegiance) deserved exemption from tribute to the high king at Tara. Columcille prevailed; no man could stand up to him. Also on the agenda was a proposal to suppress the order of bards, admittedly a troublesome lot, whose satires were potent enough to kill and who took the most presumptuous advantage wherever they happened to camp. Poetry, said Columcille (who was himself the most accomplished poet of his day) was an essential part of Irish life: Ireland could not be Ireland without it. Do not banish the bards, only command that they widen their circle and teach others what they know. An irresistible proposal from an irresistible humanist. As Columcille's proposal carried the assembly, twelve hundred merry bards crowded into the meeting, singing the praises of the saint, who, red-faced, pulled to his chin the cowl of his white wool cloak in order to hide his embarrassment.

Toward the end of his life, he began to have premonitions of his death. One day, he bade farewell to each of his brothers, who were out working the fields, and to the much-loved old packhorse that the monks used to cart their milk. For his last task on earth, he chose to sit down and continue his work of copying a manuscript. Writing out Psalm 34 he stopped after completing the words "But they that seek the Lord shall not want any thing that is good." He set down his quill and whispered: "Let Baithene write the rest." That night Columcille rose as usual from his spartan bed to join the brothers in singing the midnight office. As the monks reached the darkened church, they found Columcille in ecstasy before the altar. He blessed them all and died.

"He was," wrote the British historian Kathleen Hughes, "a man of the very highest birth, with all the natural advantage of command which such a circumstance gave in an aristocratic society. He had the gift of second sight, combined with a power to control other men by the force of his own personality. He was a shrewd judge of character, and yet at the same time a man of warm sympathies. His monks, the laity, even the animals felt his attraction. He could terrify, he could comfort, he could delight." This warrior-monk, this *homme de fer,* as the French monastic historian Jean Decarreaux has called him, had created by his singular determination a literate, Christian society among the Scots and Picts of northern Britain; and now, after his death, a fresh wave of his stout-hearted sons began to effect the same transformation among the pagan Angles of Northumbria from their new (but soon to be fabulous) island monastery of Lindisfarne, under the direction of Columcille's greatest spiritual heir, Aidan. As Columcille had baptized Scotland—and taught it to read—Aidan would do the same for all of northern England.

And just as the unyielding warrior Cuchulainn had served as the model of prehistoric Irish manhood, Columcille now became the model for all who would earn the ultimate victory. Monks began to set off in every direction, bent on glorious and heroic exile for the sake of Christ. They were warrior-monks, of course, and certainly not afraid of whatever monsters they might meet. Some went north, like Columcille. Others went northwest, like Brendan the Navigator, visiting Iceland, Greenland, and North America, and supping on the back of a whale in mid-ocean. Some set out in boats without oars, putting their destination completely in the hands of God. Many of the exiles found their way to continental Europe, where they were more than a match for the barbarians they met. They, whom the Romans had never conquered (and evangelized only, as it were, by accident in the person of Patrick, the imperfect Roman), fearlessly brought the ancient civilization back to its ancient home.

One of these erratic travelers was Columbanus, twenty years or so the junior of Columcille, born in the province of Leinster about the year 540, and subsequently a monk at Bangor for twenty-five years. About 590 he departed, with the requisite twelve companions, for Gaul, where he founded in quick succession three forest monasteries among the barbarous Sueves—Annegray, Fontaines, and Luxeuil, one of the most important foundations of the early Middle Ages. Such astounding activity could only mean that Columbanus was having similar success to Columcille in attracting local talent.

But before long he clashes with the region's bishops, who are nettled by his presence. Still employing the old Roman episcopal pattern of living urbanely in capital cities and keeping close ties with those who wear crowns, the bishops tend their local flocks of literate and semiliterate officials, the ghostly remnants of the lost society. It has never occurred to these churchmen to venture beyond a few well-tended streets into the rough-hewn mountain settlements of the simpler Sueves. To Columbanus, however, a man who will take no step to proclaim the Good News beyond the safety and comfort of his own elite circle is a poor excuse for a bishop. In 603 the bishops summon the saint to appear before them in synod at Chalon-sur-Saône. Columbanus, who cannot be bothered to take part in such a travesty, sends a letter in his stead—a letter calculated to send the bishops right up their well-plastered walls:

To the holy lords and fathers—or, better, brothers—in Christ, the bishops, priests, and remaining orders of holy church, I, Columba the sinner, send greeting in Christ:

I give thanks to my God that for my sake so many holy men have gathered together to treat of the truth of faith and good works, and, as befits such, to judge of the matters under dispute with a just judgment, through senses sharpened to the discernment of good and evil. Would that you did so more often!

The Irishman goes on to take the bishops to task for their worldly laxity and lack of industry and for trifling with his mission. They have more than enough to concern them, without sticking their episcopal noses into his affairs, if only they took their own responsibilities seriously. He couches his criticisms in the language of deference ("if you are willing for us juniors to teach you fathers"), but there is no mistaking his meaning. He recommends his own way of life to their reverences ("if we all choose to be humble and poor for Christ's sake") and urges them, after "the Gospel saying," to become as little children: "For a child is humble, does not harbor the remembrance of injury, does not lust after a woman when he looks on her, does not keep one thing on his lips and another in his heart." It almost sounds as if the saint knows each bishop's secret sin—and means to push it in his face.

Needless to say, he wins no friends at the synod, and when Columbanus attracts the enmity of Brunhilda, the wicked Visigothic princess who rules Burgundy, the bishops conspire with her to have Columbanus deported. Columbanus and his Irish monks are forced to bid farewell to their thriving communities, now populated with local Germanic monks, and to travel under royal escort to Nantes, the port from which they will be put on board a ship bound for Ireland. On their way to Nantes, one of their number, the aged Deicola, finds that he cannot keep up. He drops behind and builds himself a hut in the wilderness at a place called Lure, which will become in time another historic monastery. When Columbanus's party is at last put on board the ship at Nantes, the ship sinks, and Columbanus and four companions escape. Now a double exile (from Burgundian Gaul as well as Ireland), Columbanus means to make his way to northern Italy to convert the Lombards. But while journeying over the Alps, he is forced to stop at Arbon, near Bregenz on Lake Constance, because Gall, his expert in Germanic languages, falls ill with fever and refuses to go farther. After a heated altercation, Columbanus leaves Gall behind, and with his remaining companions heads for the plain of Lombardy, where they will build at Bobbio the first Italo-Irish monastery. Vigorous Columbanus, now in his early seventies, takes his part in the construction, happily carrying wooden beams on his shoulders.

The year of Columbanus's arrival in Lombardy was 612. In the following year, his old enemy Brunhilda is overthrown and brutally executed by the Frankish nobility. Clothaire of Neustria, who was always a friend to Columbanus and now holds sway among the Franks of Burgundy, sends a deputation over the Alps, carrying chests of gold to help in the construction of Bobbio and an invitation begging Columbanus's return to Luxeuil. But the vigorous old abbot declines. He will die at Bobbio —but not before sending more letters, including a long one to Pope Boniface IV, taking him to task for failing (as Columbanus saw it) to put a proper end to the Nestorian controversy, a complex Greek dispute about the "natures" of Christ that Columbanus may not have understood. He even makes a pun on the name of Boniface's predecessor, Pope Vigilius: *"Vigila, atque quaeso, papa, vigila, et iterum dico, vigila; quia forte non bene vigilavit Vigilius"* ("Be vigilant then, I implore you, pope, be vigilant, and again do I say, be vigilant; since perhaps he who was called Vigilant was not"). This was not Columbanus's first letter to a pope—nor even the first time he had made light of a pope's name! In a letter to Pope Gregory the Great at the time of his disputes with the bishops, Columbanus had written most familiarly—as if he were an intimate old friend—and had made a pun on the name of Gregory's predecessor Leo the Great, reminding Gregory of the scripture that "a living dog is better than a dead lion [*Leo* in Latin]." In response to each of these letters Columbanus received only cold pontifical silence.

This swaggering behavior has confounded historians, prompting them to wonder if Columbanus was a little off his rocker. But I think we may chalk up his attitude to his Irishness. (He even boasts to Boniface of "the freedom of discussion characteristic of my native land.") In chilly, cityless Ireland, men worked in close cooperation by day and slept side by side at night. Even the king was one's intimate—and the Irish word *ri* suggests an intimacy that could never be imagined of *rex*. To Columbanus, the pope was one of the brothers, a father abbot worthy of respect, by all means—but also in need, like any man, of an occasional jab in the ribs. The jab might even be one's religious duty, in a manner of speaking.

Any question of Columbanus's balance is swept away when you take a serious look at his achievements: at his death in 615 he left behind a considerable body of work—letters and sermons, notable for their playful imitation of such classical writers as Sappho, Virgil, Ovid, Juvenal, Martial, and even Ausonius; instructions for the brethren; poems and lyrics, including a jolly boat song; and the even larger legacy of his continental monasteries, busily engaged in reintroducing classical learning to the European mainland. At this great distance in time, we can no longer be sure exactly how many monasteries were founded in Columbanus's name during his lifetime and after his death. But the number, stretching across vast territories that would become in time the countries of France, Germany, Switzerland, and Italy, cannot be less than sixty and may be more than a hundred—enough to fill a page or two of this book. He had been on the continent for just twenty-five years.

One monastery on which we have some information is that of Saint Gall in the Alps, founded by the monk Columbanus had quarreled with and who went on to become the central figure in the founding of the Swiss church. Finding himself, after Columbanus's huffy departure, alone among wolves, bears, and illiterate Alemans, Gall, a more patient man than Columbanus, went about visiting his neighbors, instructing them in faith and letters. We possess only one work from his hand, a sermon of such honesty, simplicity, and generosity that we can still grasp what touched the Alemans. In 615, as Columbanus lay dying, there came a knock on Gall's door: brethren from Bobbio had arrived with Columbanus's abbatial staff, Columbanus's tardy apology, and implicit acknowledgment that Gall was the greatest of all his spiritual sons. In 616, Gall, whose labors were becoming well known, refused the offer to become bishop of Constance and in 627 the invitation to return to flourishing Luxeuil as its abbot. He stuck to his task, and by his death in 645 all of the Alemans had received the

Gospel. But he could little know that after he was long dead there would rise on the site of his labors one of the greatest of all medieval monasteries, named in his honor. In the ninth century, one of his spiritual sons, a Leinsterman, sitting in the now enormous scriptorium of the towering monastery on Lake Constance, would put together a commonplace book containing bits of all his favorite reading—notes from a commentary on the *Aeneid,* excerpts from Jerome and Augustine, some Latin hymns, a little Greek, some idiosyncratic natural history, and in Irish his own perfect poem about his cat, Pangur Ban. Thinking no doubt of his Irish home, the scribe also writes down this sentence from Horace: *"Caelum non animum mutant qui trans mare current"* ("They change their sky but not their soul who cross the ocean"). A good maxim for all exiles and, in this context, a reminder of the constancy of Irish personality.

There is much we do not know about these Irish exiles. Their clay and wattle buildings have long since disappeared, and even most of their precious books have perished. But what they knew—the Bible and the literatures of Greece, Rome, and Ireland—we know, because they passed these things on to us. The Hebrew Bible would have been saved without them, transmitted to our time by scattered communities of Jews. The Greek Bible, the Greek commentaries, and much of the literature of ancient Greece were well enough preserved at Byzantium, and might be still available to us *somewhere*—if we had the interest to seek them out. But Latin literature would almost surely have been lost without the Irish, and illiterate Europe would hardly have developed its great national literatures without the example of Irish, the first vernacular literature to be written down. Beyond that, there would have perished in the west not only literacy but all the habits of mind that encourage thought. And when Islam began its medieval expansion, it would have encountered scant resistance to its plans—just scattered tribes of animists, ready for a new identity.

Whether this state of affairs would have been better or worse than what did happen, I leave to the reader to ponder. But what is certain is that the White Martyrs, clothed like druids in distinctive white wool robes, fanned out cheerfully across Europe, founding monasteries that would become in time the cities of Lumièges, Auxerre, Laon, Luxeuil, Liège, Trier, Würzburg, Regensburg, Rheinau, Reichenau, Salzburg, Vienna, Saint Gall, Bobbio, Fiesole, and Lucca, to name but a few. "The weight of the Irish influence on the continent," admits James Westfall Thompson, "is incalculable." Saint Fursa

The most important centers of Irish-Christian influence

the Visionary went from Ireland to East Anglia, then to Lagny, just east of Paris, then to Péronne, which would be known in time as *Peronna Scottorum,* Péronne of the Irish and City of Fursey. Caidoc and Fricor advanced on Picardy. Virgil the Geometer, an Irish satirist, became archbishop of Salzburg. The scholar Donatus, according to his epitaph, "Scottorum sanguine creatus" ("born of Irish blood"), was chosen in a popular election to be bishop of Fiesole, where he ruled for nearly fifty years. Saint Cathal (or Cahill, to use the modern spelling), widely venerated to this day in southern Italy as San Cataldo, was surprised on his way back from pilgrimage in the Holy Land to find himself elected bishop of Taranto, a city on the arch of Italy's boot. Women exiles went forth as well; and though we know even less about them than we know about the men, the continental churches dedicated to Brigid in France, Germany, Austria, and Italy offer some evidence of their presence. At Amay in Belgium there was even discovered in 1977 a sarcophagus, ornamented in the Celtic manner and showing the image of a woman (mysteriously labeled "Saint Chrodoara") who carries a bishop's crozier. More than half of all our biblical commentaries between 650 and 850 were written by Irishmen. Before the end of the eighth century, the exiles had reached Modra in Moravia, where an old church has been dug up that looks just like the little church at Glendalough; and there are traces of the White Martyrs as far as Kiev. But an adequate list of missionaries and their foundations would fill another chapter. Suffice it to say that as late as 870, Heiric of Auxerre can still exclaim in his *Life of Saint Germanus:* "Almost all of Ireland, despising the sea, is migrating to our shores with a herd of philosophers!"

By this point, the transmission of European civilization was assured. Wherever they went the Irish brought with them their books, many unseen in Europe for centuries and tied to their waists as signs of triumph, just as Irish heroes had once tied to their waists their enemies' heads. Wherever they went they brought their love of learning and their skills in bookmaking. In the bays and valleys of their exile, they reestablished literacy and breathed new life into the exhausted literary culture of Europe.

And that is how the Irish saved civilization.

The End
of the
World

Is There Any Hope?

At Pentecost of 597, just days before the mighty Columcille breathed his last in his island monastery of Iona, an English king was baptized in his capital of Canterbury by a timid Roman librarian, whom Gregory the Great had sent to evangelize the English.⁑ Though Patrick had brought the Gospel to the Irish more than a century and a half earlier and Columcille had departed to the Scots forty years previously, this is the first instance of a papal mission to the pagans. Thus begins a new chapter in the story of Britain, whose first Christian inhabitants —the Celtic Britons of Patrick's day—had been gradually pushed westward by those marauding pagan adventurers, the Angles, Saxons, and Jutes, who had at length settled down to call east Britain their own. By the time of Columcille's death, these Germanic settlers were long established in southern Britain, which they now called England, and had given their home territories new names, like Kent, Essex (East Saxony), Wessex (West Saxony), and Sussex (South Saxony). They continued to push the Celtic Britons ever westward—onto the Cornish peninsula and past the river Severn into Wales. In the far north they pressed beyond Hadrian's Wall and as far as the river Tweed, the border of present-day Scotland, where they established the kingdom of Northumbria. Their relentless pressure was the central

⁑ The casual Roman attitude toward slavery, in contradistinction to Patrick's, is well illustrated by the famous anecdote about Pope Gregory the Great's first encounter with Englishmen. He notices them on sale while passing through the Roman market and, taken by their blond beauty, asks what manner of men they are. *"Angli"* (Angles or Englishmen), comes the reply. Witty Gregory indulges himself in a pun, saying they are aptly named for they look like *angeli,* angels. He goes on to make two more puns and resolves to see that the English are evangelized. But he leaves the captives to be sold.

fact of life for their victims, the old Britons, who were both Celtic and Christian and who despised their pagan foe. The last thing these British Celts would have considered was to bring the Gospel to such beasts.

The Irish Celts, who had not suffered at Anglo-Saxon hands, had no such inhibitions. Just as the new English invaded the old Celtic territories, the Irish monks launched a spiritual invasion of England from their island monastery of Lindisfarne in the northeast corner of Northumbria, establishing new monasteries in brisk succession. On account of this activity, Aidan, Columcille's beloved disciple and first abbot of Lindisfarne, has far better claim than Augustine of Canterbury to the title Apostle of England, for, as the Scottish historian James Bulloch has remarked, "All England north of the Thames was indebted to the Celtic mission for its conversion." Nor was Lindisfarne the only launching pad for the Irish monks: they were on good terms with the British Celts and began to set up bases in the western territories as well.

But the stricter Roman Christianity of Augustine's Canterbury was also slowly spreading north and west through the English territories, and was bound eventually to meet Celtic Christianity, marching in the opposite direction. A clash of custom and sensibility was as unavoidable as it had been between Columbanus and the Burgundian bishops. It came to a head at a synod, held in 664 at the Abbey of Whitby in Northumbria, at which the Northumbrian king ruled in favor of the "Roman" party—that is, the party who were heirs to Augustine's papal mission.

The main issue—as had also, by the way, been the case in the Burgundian synod—was the correct date for celebrating Easter. The Roman party thought the Celtic calculation, which differed from their own by a few days (or, in some years, weeks), tantamount to heresy. In the church's early centuries, dominated by the subtleties of Greek thought, one needed to misunderstand the exact relationship between Christ's divine and human natures or assert that he had more than one persona or something equally obscure in order to qualify as a proper heretic. The early Christian fathers could not have been bothered with anything as mundane as calendrical calculations. It is a mark of how simpleminded and inflexible the thought of the age had become that the issue of a calendar could have come so close to precipitating schism.

As it happened, the Irish party gave in—with a few holdouts who came over in time. They agreed, however reluctantly, that their father in God, Columcille, whose name was invoked in all their customs, took second place to Peter, the prince of the Lord's apostles, in whose name the Roman party made its argument. The solution, like the problem, was a simpleminded one: our relics—the bones of our founder—are holier than yours, so Rome is greater than Iona, and thus we've got right on our side.

The scene at Whitby has been used repeatedly, by both Anglicans and Roman Catholics, to defend their positions against each other, and it is almost impossible to read any historian of this period without getting a whiff of partisanship. For Anglicans, the clash proves that there was an indigenous "British" church that preceded Roman interference. For Catholics, the Celtic acquiescence is proof that, once the Celtic Christians thought things through, they saw that Rome was the necessary norm of orthodoxy. Far too much, I suspect, has been made of this clash—as much as anything because our source, Bede (a monk-historian in the early eighth century at the Northumbrian abbey of Jarrow, a satellite of Lindisfarne), makes so much of it. A man of his time (and a most seductive storyteller), Bede was, though a great admirer of Irish spirituality and learning, painfully impressed by the importance of uniformity. A more balanced perspective is suggested by Cummian, an Irish abbot who helped bring the Celtic party over to the Roman observance by humorously deprecating the Celtic argument: "What thing more perverse can be felt of our church than if we say, 'Rome is wrong, Jerusalem is wrong, Antioch is wrong, the whole world is wrong: only the Irish and the Britons know what is right, these peoples who are almost at the ends of the earth, and, you might say, a pimple on the chin of the world?' " In other words, universal opinion, not some arbitrary Roman rule, should induce the Celts to change their mind.

The trivial nature of the clash may be seen especially in the other item on Whitby's agenda—the Irish tonsure, which unlike the Roman shaved circlet at the crown of the head was achieved by shaving the front of the head from ear to ear and letting the hair in back grow long. Even to our eyes, the Irish tonsure would have a ludicrous appearance, but to the Romans it was proof of barbarian status. How could people who looked so ridiculous mean to suggest that this absurd tonsure was a sign of consecration?

What is far more impressive about the period as a whole—and perhaps even about what actually happened at Whitby—is the close fraternal cooperation between the Irish and the English. The Christian Saxons at all times received the Irish warmly as elder brothers and sisters in Christ, and borrowed generously from these generous elders. If Christians of different tribes had in all ages cooperated with one another as did these men and women, the world would be a very different place.

The Saxon monasteries, often founded by Irish monks, learned from them the scribal arts and reverence for the written word. The Lindisfarne Gospels, as consummate an example of Irish scribal art as the Book of Kells, is the work of Eadfrith, successor to Aidan as abbot of Lindisfarne, the same Eadfrith to whom Aldhelm of Malmesbury had written when he was an English student in Ireland, warning him about Irish laxity in regard to pagan literature. Though the Lindisfarne Gospels, almost the only codex for which we have a scribe's name, is the work of an Englishman, it is utterly Irish in spirit. The Saxons also absorbed the Celtic piety toward their ancestral past, and continued to tell stories of their ancient heroes. Just as the Irish did, they often reimagined these tales and gave them a Christian spin. Beowulf, the great Germano-English hero, is a pagan warrior, sure enough, but he is presented as a model of Saxon manhood—loyal, courageous, generous; and as the poet told the tale, the English Christian audience would have picked up the hints, concealed within the poet's text, that Beowulf grappling with the monsters was a type of Christ grappling with Satan. Both the Celtic and the Saxon myths and legends were becoming, in fact, secular Old Testaments, histories that lacked the direct revelations of Abraham and Moses, but symbolic salvation histories nonetheless, where one could read of a people journeying, by trial and error, prophecy and instinct, toward the truth, propelled forward through darkness and death by their own innate goodness.

The Greek approach to thought was now almost completely lost. Baptism, though it had connected the Irish to a larger world, had hardly made them Athenians. And though the Irish—and now the Saxons—succeeded in transcribing the works of ancient philosophers, they could not really understand them—nor for that matter could the few remaining Romans of the west, like Gregory the Great. The intellectual disciplines of distinction, definition, and dialectic that had once been the glory of men like Augustine were unobtainable by readers of the Dark Ages, whose apprehension of the world was simple and immediate, framed by myth and magic. A man no longer subordinated one thought to another with mathematical precision; instead, he apprehended similarities and balances, types and paradigms, parallels and symbols. It was a world not of thoughts, but of images.

Even the "Romans" at Whitby presented their point of view in the new way. They did not argue, for genuine intellectual disputation was beyond them. They held up pictures for the mind—one set of bones versus another. Indeed, the Northumbrian king, who ruled in favor of the Roman party, did so because he imagined that Peter, Rome's supposed first bishop, to whom Jesus had, in a metaphorical phrase, given "the keys to the kingdom of heaven," would use those keys to lock the king out of heaven if he ruled against Rome.

Nor did the "Romans" even trouble to draw up an extended list of charges, as would once have been the case in the church's great councils. After all, the Irish had many peculiar customs, encouraged diversity, enjoyed pagan literature far more than was good for them, were unconcerned about uniformity of monastic rule, and, perhaps worst of all, sometimes allowed a woman to rule over them. But the synod was held at Whitby, a double monastery of the Celtic style, dependent on Lindisfarne and ruled by the great abbess Hilda! The Roman party wisely confined its objections to the two matters it found most irksome because they were most *visible*. By the mid-seventh century, the visible image has assumed far greater reality than the invisible thought.

Another reason that these provincial practitioners of *Romanità* were far more circumspect than they might once have been was that the collapse of the empire and the rise of the barbarian fiefdoms had slowed communication considerably. Without the efficient communications system of the Roman Imperium, uniformity was necessarily in peril. For a century and a half—from the middle of the fifth century to the end of the sixth—there had been, so far as we can tell, no formal communication between Rome and the Christians of Britain, nor had there ever been any between Rome and Ireland— which is why the Celts were still keeping Easter according to calculations that had been twice superseded at Rome. On these marginal islands, who could know for sure what was in, what was out in Rome, let alone in the other ancient centers of Christianity? It was a great moment for diversity, and the Irish continued to thrive.

By the second half of the seventh century the Irish missionary impulse was at high tide, supplemented in its force by fresh waves of English missionaries, who in imitation of their elder brothers burst upon the Germanic lands whence their ancestors had once come. Wilfrid, the leader of the winning party at Whitby, turned his zeal on Frisia. Willibrord founded the monastery of Echternach in Luxembourg (whence the Echternach Gospels, spectacular companion to the Lindisfarne Gospels, would spring), and he and Boniface established sees at Utrecht, Würzburg, Erfurt, Eichstadt, and Passau. Boniface founded the great abbey at Fulda, established other monasteries at Disbodenburg, Amoenaburg, Fritzlar, Buraburg, and

Heidenheim, and restored the see of Mainz, of which Boniface became archbishop. By the middle of the eighth century most of Frisia, Saxony, Thuringia, Bavaria, and part of Denmark had received the Gospel.

To many of these new foundations came the books of the insular scribes. Boniface and Alcuin (the Northumbrian monk at Charlemagne's court who in 782 took over direction of the Palatine School, which would one day turn into the University of Paris) could never find the books they needed on the continent and were always sending urgent requests to British foundations for basic works. In truth, the art of the scriptorium was virtually unknown in the indigenous monasteries of Italy and Gaul. Monastic manuscript art had traveled from the workshops of Syria and Egypt by way of Ireland and Britain and, at last, to the continent of Europe. But now, the depleted store of continental codices rose steadily. By the middle of the eighth century, Fulda, for instance, was employing forty full-time scribes.

The Irish connections of these English monks were not incidental. Besides having profited substantially from the intellectual atmosphere that the Irish foundations had established in Britain, many had studied in Ireland (Willibrord had spent twelve years there) or were assisted in their labors by Irish monks (such as Kilian and his eleven companions, who evangelized Franconia and Thuringia). Alcuin's first master, Colgu, had been Irish, as was his best friend, Joseph, who accompanied him to France and died beside him; and he was succeeded at the court school by the Irish scholar Clement Scotus.

With the advent of Charlemagne as king of the Franks and (after his surprise coronation by the pope on Christmas Day 800) Holy Roman Emperor, we can begin to speak of France, in preference to Gaul. Charlemagne presided over medieval

Europe's first Renaissance, a short-lived cultural flowering that barely outlasted his reign. His enduring influence lay in the gradual revival of literacy, for he repeatedly urged (and supported) the raising of standards in the few poor continental schools that remained. That he himself was an illiterate, who late in life laboriously learned to decipher some simple texts but could never get the hang of writing, is proof enough of the standards of the age. Without the previous (and continuing) influx of Irish codices, the Carolingian Renaissance would have been impossible. For this reason, as Charlemagne's biographer Einhard tells us, Charlemagne *"amabat peregrinos"* ("loved the wandering monks").

They seemed, indeed, to be everywhere. When Charlemagne found himself puzzling over what a solar eclipse might be, Dungal, an Irish recluse at Saint Denis, was invited to instruct the king in these abstruse matters, which he did in a letter we still possess. Another resident at the Frankish court was the Irishman Dicuil, the first medieval geographer, whose cold-eyed skepticism and wry asides in his *Measurement of the Globe* still make entertaining reading. Yet another Irish courtier was Sedulius Scotus, a diverting Ciceronian who advised the emperor on statecraft and whose verses the Empress Ermingarde worked as samplers. Sedulius copied out three manuscripts that we still possess: a Greek psalter in the Arsenal Library at Paris, an interlinear Greek/Latin version of the Gospels at Saint Gall, and the Codex Boernerianus at Dresden, which is an interlinear version of Paul's Epistles—and which contains the little Irish poem about the unprofitability of pilgrimage to Rome (page 178), written obviously by Sedulius himself. In addition to these, either Sedulius or someone of his circle is responsible for the Saint Gall Priscian, authored by the Latin grammarian and full of juicy Irish glosses, and the Codex Bernensis, containing Horace's Odes, Servius's commentary on Virgil, and some of Augustine's early "how-to" books, written for his rhetoric students.

The most splendid blossom of this continental spring was an Irishman, John Scotus Eriugena,[*] born about 810, who crossed to France in his early thirties and took a position at the Palatine School, then under the patronage of Charlemagne's successor, Charles the Bald. John Scotus, who was probably a layman, is the first philosopher of the Middle Ages, the first truly Christian philosopher since the death of Augustine in 430, the first European philosopher since the execution of Boethius in 524, the first man in three hundred years who was able to think. He also had a vicious sense of humor, penning this two-liner on the death of the anti-Irish Hincmar, Archbishop of Rheims:

> *Hic jacet Hincmarus, cleptes vehementer avarus,*
> *Hoc solum gessit nobile: quod periit.*
> Here lies Hincmar, crook. But savage greed aside,
> He did one truly noble thing: he died.

His wine-soaked dinners with the emperor were full of parrying wit. *"Quid distat inter sottum et Scottum?"* ("What separates a fool from an Irishman?") asked the emperor playfully.

"Tabula tantum" ("Only the table"), came Eriugena's reply. No wonder there is a legend that his students finally stabbed him to death with their pens.

[*] Johannes Scotus, or John the Irishman; but since in this period many *Scoti* were born in Irish settlements outside Ireland, his name is qualified by *Eriugena,* or Irish-born. He is not to be confused with Duns Scotus, a Scottish theologian of a later period.

In his day, he was one of only two residents of western Europe known to be fluent in Greek. The other, the papal librarian Anastasius, was incredulous that "a barbarian" like Scotus Eriugena should know so much Greek. But know it he did. To read his *De Divisione Naturae (The Division of Nature)* after immersion in the folk literature we have been reading is a shocking experience: one is back in the world of Plato. Here is a mind that could grasp the most rarefied distinctions of the Greek philosophical tradition and, far more important, could elaborate a new system of thought, one that is balanced and internally consistent. It has more than a *soupçon* of Celticity in it, however, for John Scotus's favorite word is *Nature,* a word beloved of the Irish but one that never failed to raise the hackles of both Platonists and Roman Christians. In John Scotus's system *Nature* is a virtual synonym for *Reality*—all of reality, our natural world as well as the reality of God. In Scotus there is no useful distinction between natural and supernatural. Though the system is both subtle and elaborate, one sees immediately his debt to Patrick's simple worldview. Reality is a continuum, and all God's creatures are theophanies of God himself, for God speaks in them and through them.

To readers of a later, more punitive age, this would sound suspiciously like pantheism, the heresy that God is not just in all things but *is* all things—that is, that there is no distinction between God and creation. The further they read, the more unorthodox this Irishman's philosophy would appear. He boldly opposed reason to authority: "Every authority that is not confirmed by true reason seems to be weak, whereas true reason does not need to be supported by any authority." And this bit of sententiousness he dared apply to the fathers of the church! More than this, he took the perfectly orthodox statement of Paul that in the end "God will be all in all" and used it not only to prop up his pantheism but to suggest that at the end of time everyone—even the devils—will be saved! In 1225, almost four centuries after it was written, Pope Honorius III ordered all copies of *De Divisione Naturae* to be burned. Some, obviously, escaped the bonfire.

But in the age of John Scotus Eriugena, Christian churchmen did not burn books. Only barbarians did that.

Even as John Scotus was crossing to the continent from Ireland, Ireland was under siege. The Viking terrorists had discovered its peaceful monasteries, now rich in precious objects. The monks built round towers without ground-floor entrances and hauled their plate up rope ladders, which they then pulled up after themselves. But such towers were no match for Vikings, nor were the monks, by this time growing sleek and tame. Nor apparently were the warriors, many of whom had turned into relatively peaceful, even erudite, laymen. The illiterate Vikings often destroyed books by ripping off bejeweled covers for booty. The constant fear of the monks is well illustrated in this four-line gloss:

Bitter is the wind this night
Which tosses up the ocean's hair so white.
Merciless men I need not fear
Who cross from Lothland on an ocean clear.

The merciless men from Lothland—Norway—could not land in a storm, which soon became the only protection left to the coastal monks of Ireland and Britain. Attacks on magical Lindisfarne, which had become the constant source of the most exquisite of the insular codices, began in the last decade of the eighth century, as we read in *The Anglo-Saxon Chronicle* for 793: "On the sixth of the Ides of June the ravaging of the heathen men lamentably destroyed God's church at Lindisfarne." Monks were stripped and tortured; and the raiders came again in 801 to set the buildings afire, in 806 to kill scores of monks, in 867 to burn the rebuilt abbey. In 875 the harried survivors left Lindisfarne for good. In the first decade of the ninth century came the turn of Columcille's Iona, where "a great number of layfolks and clerics were massacred" in repeated raids. The great foundation had at last to be abandoned. Inis Murray was destroyed in 802, never to rise again. Even remote Skellig Michael was raided repeatedly, its harmless abbot Etgal carried off for ransom but dying "of hunger on their hands," as we read in *The Annals of Inisfallen*. Glendalough was pillaged on countless occasions and, between 775 and 1071, destroyed by fire at least nine times. Bangor, Moville, Clonfert, Clonmacnois, Brigid's Kildare—each was laid waste in turn. In 840, even the extensive buildings of Patrick's Armagh were burned to their foundations.

As one by one the great monastic *civitates* fell before the implacable Vikings, precious books and metalware were buried in haste or sent inland to some place thought to be—temporarily, at least—more secure. In this way, the greatest of all surviving Gospel codices, the Book of Kells, is thought to have been brought from imperiled Lindisfarne to the inland foundation of Kells. In modern times, and still today, a farmer's spade will occasionally uncover some lost treasure, like the Ardagh Chalice; or some noble family, reduced even to peasant status by Ireland's subsequent woeful history, will be found to have preserved through all the centuries a weathered codex as fantastic as the Cathach of Columcille.⁂

To Irish eyes, the Vikings had little to recommend them. They did establish Ireland's first genuine cities, places like Limerick, Cork, Wexford, Waterford, and Dublin. But they interrupted something that could never be resumed. When the Vikings were vanquished in the early eleventh century, Irish society recovered, in the sense that the normal business of life sprang back in expectable patterns. But Ireland would never recover its cultural leadership of European civilization. It had been marginalized once more. Nevertheless, the Irish way had already become the leaven of medieval civilization, the unidentified ingredient that suffused the bread of Europe, enabling it to

⁂ The Ardagh Chalice was discovered in 1868 (along with four brooches and a bronze cup) by a Limerick boy digging potatoes in the rath, or prehistoric fort, of Ardagh. The objects had been concealed under a stone slab within the roots of a thorn bush. We cannot know whether these were hidden during the Viking invasions or during Penal times, when liturgical vessels were outlawed by the British. The Cathach of Columcille was kept in the O'Donnell family, brought to France after the Treaty of Limerick by a fleeing O'Donnell, and returned to Ireland in the nineteenth century. Though the O'Donnells never descended to peasant status, other books were certainly preserved in such families, who sometimes valued them more for their supposed curative properties than for their antiquarian importance. One seventeenth-century traveler reports staring in horror as the priceless Book of Durrow was dipped in water by farmers who used it, as needed, to flavor a tonic for sick cows.

breathe and grow—and escape the humorless confines of Roman uniformity and classical pessimism.

Ireland's next invasion—by Normans in the twelfth century—changed little, for the Irish Normans adopted Irish customs far more eagerly than the English Normans married with indigenous Saxon culture. The Normans became, in the famous phrase, *"Hibernis Hiberniores,"* "more Irish than the Irish themselves." Subsequent invaders were not so appreciative. In the sixteenth century, the colonizing Elizabethans cut down the Irish forests (to get at the impenitent dispossessed, who harried them guerrilla-style) and contemplated genocide, after the gentle recommendation of the poet Spenser. In the seventeenth century, the Calvinist Cromwellians came close to implementing this poetic recommendation. In the eighteenth century, the spirit-crushing Penal Laws denied Catholics the rights of citizens. But it took the famines of the nineteenth century—the Great Hunger—to finish the Irish off. Nearly one million Irish people died of hunger and its consequences between 1845 and 1851, while her majesty's government sat on its hands, and another million and a half emigrated during the same period, many of these dying during the difficult passage to North America or Australia. By 1914 an additional four million had emigrated, reducing Ireland's population of 1845 by a third—to less than four and a half million. That such a fertile land should have become incapable of nourishing its beloved children is indication of the economic rape it had suffered for so many centuries. For by this time, Ireland had long been England's first colony, a Third World country at the edge of Europe. It would take the Irish cultural and political movements of the twentieth century to give back to this devastated population a semblance of its self-respect.📖

If the Vikings lost Ireland its leadership role, the Penal Laws very nearly destroyed its identity. These crushing, anti-Catholic statutes ensured that virtually all the remaining native nobility would flee their ancestral land. By the end of the eighteenth century, the flight was complete. Art O'Leary was one of the last noblemen to continue to maintain a home in Ireland—and we saw in Chapter 3 what happened to him. Ireland's loss was other nations' gain: names like Hennessy (the cognac people), Lally, MacMahon, and Walsh in France; Murphy, Kindelan, Mahoney, and O'Brien in Spain; Taafe and Hegerty in Austria; O'Neill in Portugal; O'Rorke in Russia; O'Higgins in Chile; and O'Farrill in Mexico give some indication of where these Wild Geese (as they were called) fled. For the impoverished peasants who remained behind, the ruined woods and despoiled castles of Ireland were elegiac reminders of a glorious past, now peopled by aristocratic ghosts, as in the anonymous "Kilcash":

📖 The Irish have been called "Queen Victoria's most loyal subjects," because in modern times they have sometimes been —paradoxically, given their earlier history—associated with prudishness and sexual repression. This new behavior grew, I think, from the understandable anxiety of dispossessed peasants for respectability, an anxiety that surfaced, according to Frank O'Connor, "the moment English became the accepted language." Languages bring values with them, and the English that the Irish finally learned was the little queen's. But, says O'Connor, wherever the Irish language held strong, both men and women continued to regard "sexual relations as the most entertaining subject for general conversation." (The fertility festival, for instance, which was mentioned in Chapter 6, continued to be held throughout Victoria's reign in Irish-speaking Kilorglin, County Kerry.) Anyone who has visited Ireland in recent years will have noticed that the Irish are reverting to their ancient ways.

What shall we do for timber?
The last of the woods is down.
Kilcash and the house of its glory
And the bell of the house are gone,
The spot where that lady waited
Who shamed all women for grace
When earls came sailing to greet her
And Mass was said in the place.

My grief and my affliction
Your gates are taken away,
Your avenue needs attention,
Goats in the garden stray.
The courtyard's filled with water
And the great earls where are they?
The earls, the lady, the people
Beaten into the clay.

But we cannot leave the Irish beaten into the clay. In all disasters, Patrick would insist, there is ground for hope. Kilcash, whose ruined tower still stands against the Tipperary sky, was a castle of the Anglo-Norman Butler family, whose descendant William Butler Yeats would one day bring such honor to Ireland as the greatest poet of the twentieth century. Our greatest novelist, James Joyce, was reared in Dublin, Viking stronghold and provincial British capital.

Even at their lowest point, the Irish kept the candle of hope burning. In 1843, just before the famines began, a smug German traveler was startled to find evidence of learning in peasant Ireland:

I have already mentioned the somewhat antiquated learning, even of the lower classes of the people of Kerry; and now I met with a remarkable instance of it. In the bow of the boat sat a Kerryman, reading an old manuscript, which was written in the Irish language, and in the Celtic character. . . .

Some, the man told me, he had added himself; some he had inherited from his father and grandfather; and some had, in all probability, been in his family long before then. I asked him what were its contents. "They are," he answered, "the most beautiful old Irish poems, histories of wonderful events, and treatises of antiquity; for instance, the translation of a treatise by Aristotle on some subject of natural history."

I don't know what it does to you, dear Reader, but the unlikely survival of an Irish codex in the gnarled hands of a Kerry farmer sends shivers up my spine.

As we, the people of the First World, the Romans of the twentieth century, look out across our Earth, we see some signs for hope, many more for despair. Technology proceeds apace, delivering the marvels that knit our world together—the conquering of diseases that plagued every age but ours and the consequent lowering of mortality rates, revolutions in crop yields that continue to feed expanding populations, the contemplated "information highway" that will soon enable all of us to retrieve information and communicate with one another in ways so instant and complete that they would dazzle those who built the Roman roads, the first great information system.

But that road system became impassable rubble, as the empire was overwhelmed by population explosions beyond its borders. So will ours. Rome's demise instructs us in what inevitably happens when impoverished and rapidly expanding populations, whose ways and values are only dimly understood, press up against a rich and ordered society. More than a billion people in our world today survive on less than $370 a year, while Americans, who constitute five percent of the world's population, purchase fifty percent of its cocaine. If the world's population, which has doubled in our lifetime, doubles again by the middle of the next century, how could anyone hope to escape the catastrophic consequences—the wrath to come? But we turn our backs on such unpleasantness and contemplate the happier prospects of our technological dreams.

What will be lost, and what saved, of our civilization probably lies beyond our powers to decide. No human group has ever figured out how to design its future. That future may be germinating today not in a boardroom in London or an office in Washington or a bank in Tokyo, but in some antic outpost or other—a kindly British orphanage in the grim foothills of Peru, a house for the dying in a back street of Calcutta run by a fiercely single-minded Albanian nun, an easygoing French medical team at the starving edge of the Sahel, a mission to Somalia by Irish social workers who remember their own Great Hunger, a nursery program to assist convict-mothers at a New York prison—in some unheralded corner where a great-hearted human being is committed to loving outcasts in an extraordinary way.

Perhaps history is always divided into Romans and Catholics—or, better, catholics. The Romans are the rich and powerful who run things their way and must always accrue more because they instinctively believe that there will never be enough to go around; the catholics, as their name implies, are universalists who instinctively believe that all humanity makes one family, that every human being is an equal child of God, and that God will provide. The twenty-first century, prophesied Malraux, will be spiritual or it will not be. If our civilization is to be saved—forget about our civilization, which, as Patrick would say, may pass "in a moment like a cloud or smoke that is scattered by the wind"—if *we* are to be saved, it will not be by Romans but by saints.

Pronunciation Guide to Key Irish Words

Though Irish today is commonly written with accents (to distinguish long from short vowels), I have omitted these for simplicity's sake. The pronunciations that follow are only approximations. *Ch* in Irish has a guttural sound, as in German, Yiddish, and Hebrew. In this guide, it is shown as *ḥ*. *Gh* is also guttural, but softer—so soft that for our purposes it can be sounded simply as *h*.

Ailil	*ahl*-il
Amhairghin	*av*-ar-hin
anmchara	an–m-*ḥa*-ra
Armagh	ar-*mah*
Cathach	*ka*-haḥ
Columbanus	koll–m-*bah*-nus
Columcille	*koll*-m-kill
Conaill	*konn*-l
Conchobor	*konn*-r
Connacht	*konn*-aḥt, or *konn*-it

Cruachan Ai	*kroo*-ah-ḥan ee
Cuailnge	*kool*-ee
Cuchulainn	koo-*ḥool*-n
Derdriu	*dare*-dru, or *deer*-dr
Emain Macha	*ev*-n *ma*-ḥa
Leinster	*lehn*-ster
Medb	methv, or mayv
Noisiu	*noy*-shoo
Rathcroghan	rath-*cro*-han
Samain	*sow*-n (first syllable as in *sour*)
Tain Bo Cuailnge	toyn boe *kool*-ee
Uisliu, Uisnech	*ish*-lu, *ush*-neḥ

Bibliographical
Sources

I find myself dissatisfied with most bibliographies, because I often can't figure out which of the many books an author lists were important to him, and which were not. So, rather than list every book I consulted, I'd prefer to tell you about the ones I found especially valuable. Of course, some of the most deeply held things are sourceless—or, rather, one can no longer remember where one first learned them. They are like the radiation left over from the Big Bang—general, constant, and unplaceable.

INTRODUCTION

The Betjeman allusion is to his poem "Sunday in Ireland": "Stone-walled cabins thatched with reeds, / Where a Stone Age people breeds / The last of Europe's stone age race." Newman's story of the Lion and the Man is from Lecture I of his *Lectures on the Present Position of Catholics in England* (1851).

I: The End of the World

In English, the principal contemporary commentators on late antiquity are Peter Brown and Henry Chadwick. Brown's *The World of Late Antiquity* (London, 1971) and Chadwick's *The Early Church* (Harmondsworth and New York, 1967; in the Pelican History of the Church series) both proved helpful. Sometimes better for my purposes—because so detailed—were studies by the turn-of-the-century Irish historian Sir Samuel Dill, especially *Roman Society in the Last Century of the Western Empire* (London and New York, 1906). It is instructive to observe how little the general shape of historical interpretation has changed since Dill's time and how much contemporary historians remain in his debt.

Gibbon can be fun, at least in Book I of *The History of the Decline and Fall of the Roman Empire* (available in many editions) —after which he huffs and puffs a great deal. But every reader owes it to himself to read at least Gibbon's scandalous Chapters 15 and 16 on the rise of Christianity. *Great Issues of Western Civilization,* edited by Brian Tierney, Donald Kagan, and L. Pearce Williams (New York, 1992), has a unit called *The Decline and Fall of the Roman Empire* (previously published as a separate pamphlet, New York, 1967), which gives an admirably compact overview of current theories. Whenever large historical movements are at issue, I find myself wanting to consult *The Rise of the West: A History of the Human Community* by William McNeill (Chicago, 1963), whose interpretation of events I invariably find illuminating.

The poems of Ausonius are available in a volume of the

Loeb Classical Library and his letters in another. The translations of his poetry in this chapter are mine.

The Barbarian Kings by Lionel Casson in the *Treasures of the World* series (Chicago, 1982), provided me with the anecdote about Alaric.

II: What Was Lost

Augustine's *Confessions* are available in many editions. Frank Sheed's (London and New York, 1943) has generally been considered the best English translation, but a fresh translation has recently been made by Henry Chadwick (Oxford, 1991). The standard life is *Augustine of Hippo* by Peter Brown (California, 1967), and it is a masterpiece both of sympathy and historical interpretation. Brown is an offshoot of the (largely French) movement to recover the teachings of the fathers of the church, and his work is somewhat dependent on the earlier work of such scholars as Chene, Congar, and especially Courcelle, all of whom he credits amply. I believe the first analysis of Augustine's *Confessions* as initiating a revolution in consciousness is to be credited to Georg Misch in his unparalleled multivolume life's work, *Geschichte der Autobiographie* (Bern and Frankfurt, 1907–69). The relevant Volume 1 (in two parts) is available in English translation as *The History of Autobiography in Antiquity*.

The best translation of the *Aeneid* in English is probably Fitzgerald's. Mandelbaum's is also much admired. As for Plato, Jowett's translations (which I used) can be highly recommended, as well as Cornford's of *The Republic*. The translations from Virgil and Augustine in this chapter are mine—but with an eye to the standard translations.

On the historical evolution of the Catholic bishopric, I consulted *inter alia* two admirable books by Raymond E. Brown, *Priest and Bishop* (Paramus, 1970) and *The Churches the Apostles Left Behind* (New York, 1984); Patrick Granfield, "Episcopal Elections in Cyprian: Clerical and Lay Participation" *(Theological Studies* 37, 1976); and Alexandre Faivre, *Naissance d'une hiérarchie* (Paris, 1977).

Augustine's *The City of God* is available in several editions, both complete and abridged. An excellent abridged paperback edition is published by Image/Doubleday (New York, 1958).

III: A SHIFTING WORLD OF DARKNESS

The quotations in this chapter are largely from Thomas Kinsella's translation of the *Tain* (Oxford, 1970). The other quotations are from Amhairghin's poem, translated by Proinsias Mac-Cana in his *Celtic Mythology* (London, 1968) and from "The Lament for Art O'Leary" in *Kings, Lords, and Commons: An Anthology from the Irish,* translated by Frank O'Connor (Dublin, 1970).

IV: GOOD NEWS FROM FAR OFF

Alas! when it comes to Patrick, no one agrees with anyone about anything, and rare is the Patrician scholar who shows aught but scorn for anyone's opinions but his own. There is not a datum of Patrick's life that has not been questioned, including his existence. During the course of the twentieth century, moreover, the library of Patrician studies has grown into "a mountain of Himalayan proportions," to quote E. A. Thompson.

But the truth is that for our purposes much of this contentious scholarship can be bracketed because, thanks to the *Confession* and the *Letter,* we know far more about Patrick than about any other British or Irish figure of the fifth century. I have given the particulars of his story in a way that makes sense to me, but I would hardly urge that the choices I have made from among the many and convoluted theories are better than anyone else's. No one can claim to know for certain his dates or the dates of his travels; where in Ireland he served as a slave; where the ship that he fled in set sail from or landed or what kind of cargo it carried, if any; where he studied for the priesthood; whether he himself consecrated bishops, either as contemporaries or successors (though there can be no doubt that his episcopacy was followed by others'). But none of these problems can cast any shadow on Patrick's essential character, which shines out from his two surviving works. There is also much speculation as to the actual (as opposed to legendary) effect of his mission—though I believe that if there were some subsequent figure more responsible than Patrick for the Christianization of Ireland there would be some record of (at least) his or her name.

I have deliberately omitted from the main text any mention of Palladius, a bishop who preceded Patrick in Ireland, because I believe he has no relevance to our story. He was sent by Pope Celestine to "the Irish who believe in Christ," probably a small colony of Britons, and died in all likelihood within a couple of years of his commissioning. He was not a traveling missionary bishop, since there were none before Patrick—not just in Ireland but anywhere. It is sometimes claimed that Ulfilas, an

Arian bishop among the Germans, was a missionary bishop. But E. A. Thompson (see below), who has probably studied the matter more deeply than anyone, insists that Ulfilas was a bishop resident among believers—quite a more domestic figure than Patrick.

Patrick's first biographer was Muirchu, who wrote two centuries after Patrick's time. His *Life*, as well as Patrick's *Confession* and *Letter*, is contained in A. B. E. Hood's *St Patrick: His Writings and Muirchu's "Life"* (London and Chichester, 1978). The standard Latin text of Patrick's writings, however, is Ludwig Bieler's *Libri Epistolarum Sancti Patricii Episcopi,* which first appeared in *Classica et Mediaevalia,* 11 (1950) and 12 (1951) and is available in reprint editions. I would also recommend R. P. C. Hanson and Cecile Blanc's wonderfully informative French edition *Saint Patrick: Confession et Lettre a Coroticus* (Paris, 1978) in the magnificent series Sources Chrétiennes. The translations from Patrick's works in the course of this chapter are mine.

In this century, J. B. Bury set a high standard for Patrician scholarship with *The Life of St Patrick and His Place in History* (London, 1905). (It was he who came up with the theory of the "desert" being the result of the Germanic invasion of Gaul in 406–7.) He was followed by many others, including Eoin MacNeill in his admirable if overly pious *St Patrick, Apostle of Ireland* (London, 1934). But a paper by the legendary Patrick D. A. Binchy, "Patrick and His Biographers, Ancient and Modern" in *Studia Hibernica* 2 (1962), which blew holes in Bury's (and everyone else's) approach, is rightly considered the watershed event of modern Patrician studies. Hanson's *St Patrick: His Origins and Career* (Oxford, 1968), following on Binchy, is at present the standard life. It contains, like all its predecessors, long passages of untranslated Latin. The best life of Patrick for those who read no Latin is Thompson's entertaining *Who Was Saint Patrick?* (London, 1985; New York, 1986). Thompson's *The Visigoths in the Time of Ulfilas* (Oxford, 1966) is also splendid.

The translation of Patrick's "Breastplate" was made by Whitley Stokes, John Strachan, and Kuno Meyer and is contained in Meyer's *Selections from Ancient Irish Poetry* (London, 1911) and in many anthologies. With an eye to other translations (and what I believe to have been the author's meaning), I have revised their "spells of women" to read "spells of witches."

V: A SOLID WORLD OF LIGHT

This is the sort of chapter that could drive a careful scholar to drink. I am going here largely on supposition and insight. Our information about what was happening in Ireland just prior to Patrick's arrival is extremely slight, and our most solid information on Patrick's doings comes from his own pen. Whatever he doesn't tell us we must leave pretty much to speculation.

We know—from Julius Caesar and other ancient witnesses and from incontrovertible archaeological evidence—that the Celts practiced human sacrifice. There is no reason to think that the Irish had stopped this practice before Patrick. Since we know that culture changed little in Ireland over many centuries, the likelihood is that human sacrifice was still being carried out in Patrick's day. But we have no direct proof. Let's assume for a moment that it had died out. Its memory would nonetheless be still vivid, and the frame of mind that encouraged it would hardly have vanished, given the tenaciousness of folk custom. So, even if human sacrifice had somehow been abolished, I believe my theory of how Patrick connected imaginatively with the Irish still stands.

The information on Lindow Man comes from Anne Ross and Don Robins, *The Life and Death of a Druid Prince* (London, 1989). The standard work on ancient Celtic religious practice is Stuart Piggott, *The Druids* (London, 1974). The definitive study of Irish mythology is by Alwyn Rees and Brinley Rees in their *Celtic Heritage: Ancient Tradition in Ireland and Wales* (London, 1961). MacCana *(supra)* is also very helpful.

The translation of the hymn from Philippians is mine.

VI: WHAT WAS FOUND

The sources for this chapter are many and various. The best treatment I found of the overall subject was John T. McNeill (father of William), *The Celtic Churches* (Chicago, 1974), though he is much indebted (as am I) to the work of Kathleen Hughes, especially her unsurpassed *The Church in Early Irish Society* (London, 1966). Two books by Walter Horn, *The Forgotten Hermitage of Skellig Michael* (Berkeley, 1990) and *The Plan of St. Gall* (California, 1979), the second a quite formidable work in three volumes written with Ernest Born, are wonderful explorations of individual monastic foundations. A dissertation by the Benedictine Joseph P. Fuhrmann at Catholic University in Washington, D.C., submitted in 1927 under the title *Irish Medieval Monasteries on the Continent,* was the only study I could find devoted exclusively to this subject. A more extensive one is sorely needed!

Also helpful were Liam de Paor, *Saint Patrick's World* (Notre Dame, 1993); Jean Decarreaux, *Les Moines et la civilization* (Paris, 1962); Robin Flower, *The Irish Tradition* (Oxford, 1947), an indispensable classic; James Westfall Thompson, *The Medieval Library* (Chicago, 1939); and, for the Irish penitential movement, John Mahoney, *The Making of Moral Theology* (Oxford, 1987). Three essay collections also provided me with some useful information: *The Churches, Ireland, and the Irish,* edited by W. J. Sheils and Diana Wood (Oxford, 1989), especially "The Wild and Wooly West: Early Irish Christianity and Latin Orthodoxy" by Brendan Bradshaw; *An Introduction to Celtic Christianity,* edited by James P. Makey (Edinburgh, 1989), especially "Irish Monks on the Continent," by Tomas Cardinal O Fiaich; and *Irland und Europa,* edited by Proinseas Ni Chathain and Michael Richter (Stuttgart, 1984), especially the concluding essay, "Irland und Europa: Die Kirche im Fruhmittelalter" by Richter. This last volume, the result of the second in a series of conferences between Irish and German scholars, is full of confessions about how far scholarship in this neglected area must travel before many questions of crucial historical importance can be adequately addressed.

As for scribal and other arts, I consulted *inter alia* Françoise Henry's irreplaceable three-volume work, *Irish Art* (Ithaca, New York, 1965); Nicolete Gray, *A History of Lettering* (Boston, 1986); Christopher de Hamel, *A History of Illuminated Manuscripts* (Boston, 1986); and Michael Olmert, *The Smithsonian Book of Books* (Washington, D.C., 1992).

The reference at the beginning of the chapter to naked riders in nineteenth-century Clare originates in a wonderful talk I heard in 1970 at the Merriman Summer School given by Dr. Alf MacLochlainn, then librarian at the National Library.

The assertion that the Irish halted their international slave trade is not meant to imply that there were no slaves in Ireland after Christianity took hold. The Irish, like other medievals, kept serfs. See Nerys Patterson, *Cattle Lords and Clansmen: The Social Structure of Early Ireland* (Notre Dame, 1994). And though the Irish never resumed slave raiding, we know that during the medieval period some landholders did resume the practice of purchasing slaves from Britain, a practice that the twelfth-century Irish bishops believed brought on Ireland the divine retribution of the Norman Invasion. But this judgment implies that, even at their worst, the Christian Irish possessed a moral frame of reference superior to that of their pagan ancestors. See Donneha O Corrain, *Ireland Before the Normans* (Dublin, 1972) in the most useful Gill History of Ireland series.

VII: THE END OF THE WORLD

My sources for this chapter are, by and large, the same as for the last chapter. Bede's *Ecclesiastical History of the English People* is available in many editions. For my brief treatment of the Irish influence on the shaping and preservation of early Anglo-Saxon literature I am indebted to Charles Donahue, who was in his turn indebted to the magisterial pioneering work of J. R. R. Tolkien on the great poem *Beowulf*. Donahue's essay *"Beowulf and Christian Tradition: A Reconsideration from a Celtic Stance"* in *Traditio* 21 (1965), Fordham University's journal of "Studies in Ancient and Medieval Thought and Religion," is so discerning and generous that one hastens to recommend it as a model to those who would raise the tone and enlarge the substance of scholarship in our day.

Chronology

This is not a complete chronology, but only a list of dates relevant to historical episodes referred to in the main text. The Patrician dates are approximations.

c. 3000 B.C.   Stone Age settlers begin to construct elaborate Irish passage-graves such as Newgrange.

900s   In Greece, Homer composes *Iliad* and *Odyssey*.

753   Founding of the City of Rome.

400–300   Greece's Golden Age: the flowering of Athenian democracy under Pericles; the time of Sophocles, Phidias, Socrates, Plato, et al.

390   Celts invade the City of Rome for the first and last time.

c. 350   Celtic tribes cross to Ireland and settle there, displacing earlier inhabitants.

70 B.C.–A.D. 14   Rome's Golden Age: the time of Cicero, Catullus, Horace, Virgil, Ovid, et al.

31 B.C.	Octavian becomes first Roman emperor and takes the name Caesar Augustus.
c. A.D. 100	Medb is queen of Connacht in Ireland.
370	The teenaged Augustine goes to Carthage.
c. 395	Death of Ausonius.
401	Patricius is taken into slavery; Augustine publishes his *Confessions*.
406–7	Largest Germanic invasion of the Roman Empire.
409	Roman garrison abandons Britain.
410	Alaric the Goth sacks the City of Rome.
430	Death of Augustine at Hippo.
432	Bishop Patrick arrives in Ireland.
461	Death of Patrick.
475–76	Reign of Romulus Augustulus, the last Roman emperor, who is deposed by the barbarian Odoacer; end of the Roman Empire in the west.
c. 500	Brigid founds Kildare.
557	Columcille leaves Ireland for Iona.
c. 590	Columbanus leaves for Gaul.
597	Death of Columcille; Augustine, the papal librarian, baptizes the English king of Kent at Canterbury.
615	Columbanus dies at Bobbio.
635	Aidan founds Lindisfarne.
664	Synod of Whitby.
782	Alcuin takes over direction of Charlemagne's Palatine School.
793	First Viking attack on Lindisfarne.

c. 845	John Scotus Eriugena arrives at the court of Charles the Bald.
875	The monks abandon Lindisfarne for the last time.
1014	Vikings are defeated decisively by the forces of Brian Boru at the Battle of Clontarf.
1170	Anglo-Norman invasion of Ireland.
1556	Elizabethan plantation of Ireland begins.
1649	Cromwell arrives in Ireland and begins his massacres of Catholics.
1690	Battle of the Boyne: the Catholic (and Stuart) cause is decisively lost to the victorious William of Orange; the flight of the Wild Geese, the Irish nobility, begins soon after.
1692	Catholics are excluded from office for the first time.
1695	Penal Laws are enacted, depriving Catholics of civil rights.
1829	Daniel O'Connell, "the Liberator" and masterful Irish politician, forces Catholic Emancipation on the British Parliament.
1845	Famine. Massive emigrations begin.
1893	Douglas Hyde founds Gaelic League to revive Irish culture.
1904	William Butler Yeats and Lady Gregory found the Abbey Theatre. James Joyce leaves Ireland.
1916	Easter Rising. Irish Republic proclaimed.
1919–21	Irish War of Independence.

1922	Britain and Ireland sign treaty establishing the Irish Free State, but excluding the six counties of Northern Ireland still under British rule. *Ulysses* published.
1923	Yeats takes his seat in the first Irish Senate and is awarded the Nobel Prize for literature.

Acknowledgments

Several friends were gracious enough to read the manuscript in its various incarnations, including my wife Susan Cahill, Herman Gollub, Catherine McKenna, Jacqueline Kennedy Onassis, Michael Walsh, Maureen Waters, and Robert J. White. To them all I am most grateful, for they saved me from not a few errors and misjudgments. But I hasten to add that what errors and imbalances remain are mine alone.

Looking back over the circuitous route that brought me to this study, I find I owe an enormous debt of gratitude to teachers of long ago: John D. Boyd, S.J., who first opened up to me the élan of medieval culture; Henry Traub, S.J., whose felt appreciation for what it meant to be a Roman can be second to none; J. Giles Milhaven, who found it in his heart to take me into his exclusive Plato seminar despite my faulty Greek; and William V. Richardson, S.J., whose severe critiques of medieval philosophy in the light of modern experience enabled even his less brilliant students to reach some understanding of the philosophical process. After my student years, I had the good fortune to be befriended by the great Robert J. Pollock, the only real philosopher I have ever known and whose keen appreciation of Augustine gave impetus to my second chapter;

and by Raymond E. Brown, S.S., to my mind the greatest living American scripture scholar and whose studies of early Christian writings and society provided much inspiration and some background for my own study. Except for the last, these teachers were associated at one time or another with Fordham University, whose library—and whose librarian, James P. Mc-Cabe—were invaluable resources. Beyond all these, there is the memory of my mother, Margaret Buckley, whose sayings, stories, and songs, passed on to her by her own mother, Brigid Delia Quinn of Williamstown, County Galway, are undoubtedly the *ur*-source of this book.

I am grateful, too, to many colleagues at Bantam Doubleday Dell—more than I could possibly name here—who have cheered me on during my research and writing and whose enthusiasm for the result has been an unexpected gift. It is people like these, whether sales reps or editors, corporate officers or support staff, whose enthusiasm for *books*—even of the damnedest sort—mark them as the true successors to the Irish scribes. It is imperative that I name at least one of them, Nan Ahearn Talese. It is not often, after all, that a writer can have as his editor and publisher a combination of Medb of Cruachan, Brigid of Kildare, and the Lady of Kilcash "who shamed all women for grace."

Index

Church. *See* Catholic Church; Christianity
Cicero, 21, 46–49, 50, 58, 59, 76, 159
Cioran, Emil, 5
Circumcellions, 108
City of God, The, 13, 64
Civilisation, 4–5, 58–59
Civilization, modern, 29–30, 216–18
Civilization, Western
    Irish role in saving, 183–85, 187–88,
        192, 193–96, 205–7, 212–13
    Carolingian Renaissance, 206–10
    near-collapse of, 3–5, 58–60, 181–84,
        193–94
Clare, 149
Clark, Kenneth, 4–5, 58–59, 171
Clement Scotus, 206
Cleopatra, 23, 44
Clonfert, 211
Clonmacnois, 211
Clothaire of Neustria, 190
Codices, 160, 165, 168–69, 180, 203, 205,
    206, 207–8, 210–12, 216
Cogitosus, 175–76, 178–79
Colgu, 206
Cologne, 179–80
Columba. *See* Columcille
Columbanus, 176, 188–92
Columcille, 173, 199, 200, 201, 211
    character of, 169–70, 184–87
    emulators of, 187–88
    exile of, 170–71, 179, 183–84
    monasteries of, 184–85
Conaill, Clan, 135, 169, 170
Conchobor, 123*n*
Confession (Patrick), 104, 105*n*, 106, 113,
    134
Confessions (Augustine), 39–41, 42, 45,
    56–58
Confucius, 40
Connacht, 71, 110. *See also Tain Bo
    Cuailnge*
Constance, 192–93
Constance, Lake, 11, 190
Constantine, 28, 125, 181
Constantinople, 181
Copts, 180
Cork, 94, 212
Cornish, 79
Cornwall, 79, 158*n*
Coroticus, 110–11, 114, 134
Crimthann. *See* Columcille
Cromwell, Oliver, 213
Cruachan Ai, 71, 110
Cuailnge, 127
Cuchulainn. *See Tain Bo Cuailnge*
Cummian, 202

Curiales, 24–28, 38

Daimon, Plato on, 51–55
Dalriada, 185
Dancing at Lughnasa, 149
Danube, 11, 22
De Divisione Naturae, 209, 210
Decarreaux, Jean, 187
"Deer's Cry, The," 116–19
Deicola, 190
Delphi, 79
Demosthenes, 46, 58
Denmark, 138, 139, 142, 206
Derdriu. *See Tain Bo Cuailnge*
Derry, 170
Destruction of Da Derga's Hostel, The, 129–
    30
Diarmait, 170
Dicuil, 207
Disbodenburg, 205
Disraeli, Benjamin, 6
Division of Nature, The, 209, 210
Donatists, 64, 108
Donatus, 195
Donegal, 149
Druids, 115, 129, 131, 134, 139, 140,
    143–44, 172, 173, 177
Drumceatt, 185
Dublin, 168, 212, 215
Dungal, 207
Duns Scotus, 208*n*
Durant, Will, 49
Durrow, 169, 212*n*
Dying Gaul, 82, 97, 131

Eadfrith, 156, 203
East Anglia, 195
Easter, 116, 200–1, 205
Easter Rising, 134*n*
Echternach, 168, 205
Ecumene, 108
Egypt, 165, 180, 206
Elizabeth I, 151
Emain Macha, 109
England, 157–58, 183, 187, 199–203, 204,
    211. *See also* Britain, ancient; Great
        Britain
Eochaid Feidlech the Steadfast, 72
Epics, 43. *See also Aeneid; Tain Bo Cuailnge*
Eriugena, John Scotus, 208–10
Ermingarde, 207
Essex, 199
Etgal, 211
Euripides, 58
Europe, 11–12, 27, 180, 181. *See also*
    Civilization, Western; Roman Empire

as Celts, 78–80
character of, 148–51, 155–57
consciousness of, 126–31
customs of, 103, 149
history and, 5–8
human sacrifice by, 136–42, 148
lineages, 123*n*
literacy of, 150, 151–52, 163–65
pagan festivals of, 148–49, 214*n*
as preservers of civilization, 3–5, 183–
    85, 186–88, 194–96, 212–13
Roman prejudice against, 112–13
scholarship and, 150
secret societies, 164
sexual mores, 76–78, 110, 134–35, 149,
    178, 214*n*
war and, 82, 148, 156
See also Celts; Ireland
Isidore, 183
Islam, 180, 194
Ita, 175
Italy, 27, 28, 182–83, 190, 192, 195, 206

Jarrow, 202
Jerome, 45*n*, 47, 158–59, 193
Jesuits, 149–50
Jesus Christ, 22, 24, 47, 61, 62, 63, 105–
    6, 115–16, 123, 134*n*, 153, 165, 175,
    180, 204
    Patrick on, 132–33
    as sacrifice, 140–42
    See also New Testament
Jews, 7, 25, 30, 123*n*, 136, 137, 163, 194
John the Baptist, 123
Joseph (friend of Alcuin), 206
Joyce, James, 57, 163, 215
Judaism, 6
Julian of Eclanum, 65–66
Jutes, 158*n*, 199
Juvenal, 192

Kells, 165, 168, 169, 203, 211–12
Kennedy, John F., 97
Kent, 199
Kerry, 149, 214*n*, 216
Kevin of Glendalough, 156–58
Kiev, 195
"Kilcash," 214–15
Kilcrea Abbey, 93–94
Kildare, 173, 178–79, 185, 211
Kilian, 206
Kilorglin, 214*n*
Kingsley, Charles, 6
Kinsella, Thomas, 74

Lagny, 195

Languages, 106, 163–64
Laon, 194
Latin, 45, 46, 58, 104, 106, 160, 164, 207
Leinster, 110, 160
Leo the Great, 191
Leprechauns, 80
Lérins, 106
Letter (Patrick), 134
Lewis, C. S., 46
Leyden, 180
Libraries, 159, 168, 169, 181–82, 207
Liège, 194
Life of Saint Germanus, 195
Limerick, 142, 212
Lindisfarne, 187, 200, 202, 203, 204, 211
Lindow Man, 138, 139, 140
Lion, Newman's fable about the, 7–8
Literature
    autobiography in, 39–41
    drama, 58, 87–88, 131
    English, 79, 203
    Irish, 71–78, 80–81, 83–96, 126–31,
        132–34, 151–55, 159–64, 193, 194–
        95, 203, 207, 214–15
    poetry, 80–81, 89–93, 95–96, 129, 132–
        34, 151–55, 162–63, 186, 193, 207,
        210, 214–15
    values in, 94–97
    women in, 76, 87–93
    See also Ausonius; Augustine of Hippo,
        Saint; Civilization, Western; Plato;
        Virgil
"Little people," 80
Liverpool, 137
Loch Ness Monster, 185
Lombardy, 190
Lothland, 211. *See also* Vikings
Lough, Neagh, 101
Lovornious, 139, 140
Lug, 149
Lughnasa, 149
Lure, 190
Luxembourg, 205
Luxeuil, 188, 190, 192, 194
Lyons, 28

Machiavelli, Niccolò, 13, 14
Mahabharata, 82
Maihingen, Book of, 168
Mainz, 180, 205–6
Malraux, André-Georges, 218
Manchan of Offaly, 152–55
Manchester, 138
Mani, 49
Manicheism, 49, 50
Marcus Aurelius, 40

Maria Theresa, 92
Martial, 192
Martin of Tours, Saint, 169
Martyrdom, 151–55, 171, 172, 173, 183–84
Mary, Saint, 66
Maximus, 28
May Day, 149
Mayo, 105n
McNeill, John T., 159
McNeill, William, 18
Measurement of the Globe, 207
Medb. See Tain Bo Cuailnge
Mediterranean Sea, 12
Metalworkers, 167
Middle Ages, 27, 59–60, 133–34. See also Civilization, Western
Mil, 80–81
Milan, 22, 50, 108
Milan, Edict of, 148
Miliucc, 38, 101, 102, 103, 105n
Missionaries, 107–8, 186–96, 199, 200, 205–6. See also Monasteries; Patrick, Saint
Modra, 195
Monasteries, 169
  in Charlemagne's age, 207–8
  Columcille's, 183–85, 186–87
  conduct of, 135, 157–59, 176
  destruction by Vikings, 210–12
  founding of, 3–4, 151–55, 156–58, 171–72, 180–81, 184–85, 186–87, 189–90, 192–96, 200, 203, 205–6
  hierarchy in, 172–73
  Patrick's, 110, 135
  women in, 172–73, 174–76, 178–79, 204
  See also Missionaries; Scribes
Monica (Augustine's mother), 41, 50, 66
Moravia, 195
Moville, 170, 211
Moynihan, Daniel Patrick, 97
Munster, 110
Mythology, 22, 43, 126–27, 128–29, 130–31, 135–36, 149

Nantes, 190
Nestor, 47
Nestorians, 190
Newgrange, 167
New Hampshire, 79
Newman, John Henry, 7–8
New Testament, 24, 25, 45n, 56, 57, 61, 107, 136, 140–42, 153, 155, 159, 193, 207
New York Review of Books, The, 7

Nile Valley, 12
Normans, 213
North America, 79, 213
North Sea, 11
Northumbria, 187, 199, 200, 201, 204, 206
Norway, 211. See also Vikings
Numbers, 153

O'Connell, Daniel, 92
O'Connell, Eileen, 91–93, 94, 96
O'Connor, Flannery, 123n
O'Connor, Frank, 214n
Octavian. See Augustus
O'Donnell family, 212n
Oedipus, 130
Ogham, 164, 166
Old Life of Brigid, The, 175
Old Testament, 40, 63, 80, 86, 136, 159, 185, 193
O'Leary, Art, 91–94, 214
Oratio, 21
Oratory, 46–48
Ostrogoths, 30
Ovid, 203

Paganism, 14, 63–64, 133, 148–49
Palatine School, 206, 208
Palatine service, 26
Parentalia, 19–20
Paris, 195, 207
Paris, University of, 206
Passau, 205
Patricius. See Patrick
Patrick, 38, 39, 79, 97, 143, 168, 169, 171, 172, 179, 180, 199, 211
  bishops and, 112
  British and, 110–14, 123
  Columcille and, 185
  confession of, 106–7, 113–14, 177
  Confession, 113–14
  education of, 105, 106
  escapes slavery, 102–5
  kings and, 109–13, 115–16
  legends about, 115–16
  as missionary, 105–6, 108–16, 123–24, 126, 128, 131, 134–36, 140, 147–48, 149, 150, 151
  ordination of, 106–7
  otherworldly experiences, 102–3, 104, 105–6
  prayer of, 116–19, 131, 132–34, 143
  sexual mores and, 134–35
  as slave, 38, 39, 101–2
  slavery and, 109, 110, 112, 114, 116
  spiritual awakening, 102

and theology, 115
view of God, 131–33
view of universe, 131–34, 135–36
women and, 109
Paul, 45n, 56, 57–58, 61, 63, 79, 107, 108, 140–42
Pax Romana, 15, 29, 60–61
Pelagius, 64, 66
Penal Laws, 92, 212n, 213, 214
Pentecost, 107
Pericles, 38
Péronne, 195
Peter, 107, 181, 201, 204
Petrarch, 13, 14
Phaedrus, 51–55
Philosophy, 48–49, 65, 133, 201, 203–5, 208–10
Picts, 158n, 184, 187
Plato, 48, 50–55, 58, 59, 60, 63, 76, 107, 133
Plotinus, 58
Plunkett, Joseph, 134
Plunkett, Oliver, 134n
Porphyry, 58
Potitus, 38
Princeton University, 7
Priscian, 207
Protestants, 5, 7, 14
Pyrenees, 179

Rathcroghan, 71
Ravenna, 35
Remains, prehistoric, 138, 139–40
Renaissance, Carolingian, 206–10
Res Publica, 28
Rhetoric, 46, 48
Rhine, 11, 13, 14–15, 16–18, 22, 79, 104, 179
Robins, Don, 139
Roman Empire, 64
anti-barbarian campaigns, 22–23
army in, 26, 28–29
barbarians in, 11–18, 27, 30–31, 35, 36–37, 63, 82–83, 179–80
cities in, 107
civilization of, 38–39
consuls in, 23–24
crime in, 35–36, 37–38
fall of, 3–4, 12–14, 18, 22, 29–31, 35, 123–24, 179–80, 181, 205, 216–17
geography of, 12
law in, 60–61
learning in, 35, 38–39
offices in, 23–28
others' views of, 15, 16, 28, 30, 43–44
religion in, 22, 124–25, 148

slavery in, 37–38
social classes in, 25–28, 106, 107
taxes in, 24–28, 38
See also Ausonius; Augustine of Hippo; Civilization, Western
Roman Republic, 23, 24, 27
Romania. *See* Roman Empire
Rome (city), 22, 24, 30, 35, 43, 79, 107, 108
as holy place, 181, 201
sack of, 30–31, 35, 37, 63
Ross, Anne, 139
Rwanda, 137

Sacrifice, human, 135–43, 148
Sacrifices, animal, 136
Saint Denis, 207
Saint Gall, 192, 194, 207
"Saint Patrick's Breastplate," 116–19, 131, 132–34, 143
Salvian, 179–80
Salzburg, 194, 195
Samain, 78, 149n
Sappho, 40, 58, 192
Saul of Tarsus. *See* Paul
Saxons, 37, 79, 158n, 183, 184, 199, 202–4, 213
Saxony, 206
Scotland, 139, 171, 179, 185, 187, 199, 211
monasteries in, 171, 184–85
Scots, 80, 187
Scribes, 3–4, 183–84
artistry of, 164–67, 168–69
comments by, 160–63
on continent, 206
joy in work, 160–61, 162, 164
See also Codices; Monasteries
Scrolls, 168
Sedulius Scotus, 207–8
Senate, Roman, 25, 26
Servius, 208
Severn, 199
Seville, 183
Shamrock, 115
Shannon, William V., 147
Shape-shifting, 127, 128–30
Shepherds, 101
Sitwell, Edith, 134n
Skellig Michael, 4, 171, 211
Skeptics, 48
Slavery, 81–82, 101–2, 103, 109, 110, 112, 114, 116, 134, 148, 199n
Slavs, 60
Sliabh Mis, 101, 133
Smiths, artistry of, 167

Incipit euangelium secundum mattheu

XP
AUT
RATIONI CENERATION
ESSFISBONSATA
MATTEREUSMARIACUOZEBR